OTHER BOOKS BY AUDRE LORDE

undersong

W·W · NORTON & COMPANY · NEW YORK · LONDON

AUDRE LORDE

CHOSEN POEMS OLD AND NEW
REVISED EDITION

Some of these poems have appeared in *Heresies; The Black Scholar; The Black Collegian; The Iowa Review; Sinister Wisdom;* and *Lotus.* Others have appeared in *Black World; The Negro Digest; Seventeen Magazine; Fits; Umbra; Poetry Northeast; Parasite; Venture Magazine; Harlem Writers Quarterly; Freedomways; Massachusetts Review; Transatlantic Review; American PEN Journal; Works; Omen; Aphra; Women: A Journal of Liberation; Amazon Quarterly; Chrysalis; Ms Magazine; Painted Bride Quarterly; Squeezebox; HOODOO; Essence; Moving Out; Paunch;* and *Nimrod.*

The text of this book is composed in Garamond No. 3,
with the display set in Bellery Elongated.
Composition and manufacturing by The Maple-Vail Book Manufacturing Group.
Book design by Antonina Krass.

Library of Congress Cataloging-in-Publication Data
Lorde, Audre.
Undersong : chosen poems, old and new / Audre Lorde. — Rev. ed.
p. cm.
Rev. ed. of: Chosen poems, old and new. 1982.
I. Lorde, Audre. Chosen poems, old and new. II. Title.
PS3562.075U5 1992
811'.54—dc20   91–46706

ISBN 0-393-03395-3
W. W. Norton & Company, Inc., 500 Fifth Avenue, New York, NY 10110
W. W. Norton & Company Ltd., 10 Coptic Street, London WC1A 1PU

1 2 3 4 5 6 7 8 9 0

TO GLORIA, WITH ALL
THE TIME IN THE WORLD.

CONTENTS

Part 2

From A LAND WHERE
OTHER PEOPLE LIVE

Part 3
From NEW YORK HEAD
SHOP AND MUSEUM

Part 4

NEW POEMS 1978-1982

This volume represents revisions of the poems contained in *Chosen Poems—Old and New* (1982). Three poems have been dropped from the first edition because they required reconstruction rather than revision. Nine poems from the same time period that were not included in the earlier edition have been added because time and distance have illuminated their use.

The process of revision is, I believe, crucial to the integrity and lasting power of a poem. The problem in reworking any poem is always when to let go of it, refusing to give in to the desire to have that particular poem *do it all,* say it all, become the mythical, unattainable Universal Poem.

In order to revise effectively rather than construct a new work, one must establish the world of the poem—that constellation within emotional time and space from which the poem draws power and life. Within that world, the problem of revision is to make the poem become more itself, rather than another poem. I found this required me to propel myself back into the original poem-creating process and the poet who wrote it. Once I reestablished the world of the poem, revision served to help the poem do its work more effectively.

This is a fascinating and demanding process, one that requires reinventing the emotional climate of the often diverse experiences out of which the poem grew—recalling what the task of the poem originally was and keeping that task firmly in mind, rather than some other task the poet now might like the poem to accomplish. In other words, I set myself the task of revising, not rewriting, these poems.

This project began while I was trapped in the nightmare aftermath of Hurricane Hugo. Our house, library, and whole way of life had been destroyed in one night. While shoveling out the soaked remains of my studio, I came across a waterlogged but readable copy of *Chosen Poems,* one of the few salvageable books from my library after the storm. Weary from crisis and from lugging and hauling debris, I sat down for a few minutes and found myself reading these poems as if I were in a workshop. They were touching and powerful, but with certain nonuseful ambiguities that I would advise any young poet to reconsider in order to strengthen the poem.

If a poem has a job, how best can we help it do that job across several decades? The answers are never simple.

For every poem written, there is the bedrock of experience(s) within which the poem is anchored. A molten hot light shines up through the poem from the core of these experiences. This is the human truth that illuminates the poem, surrounding it in the light that makes it come alive.

That light can shift and alter; but if the poem is firmly anchored, it will not be quenched. How to honor that light, do justice to the subtlety of its changing auras, without shifting or fracturing the bedrock from which the poem arises—that is the task of revision: to make the poem more of what it needs to be in order to do the emotional work it was intended to do.

In order to achieve that goal, I kept two questions before me: the first, What did I want my readers to feel? and, second, What was the work of this poem (its task in the world)?

If the poem is not firmly anchored or the illumination too muddled or confused, then the poem must be reconstructed rather than revised. Hopefully, by the time a poem reaches print, it may profit from revision but does not have to be rebuilt.

In the next three months of kerosene lamps and generators, hauling water and cooking over driftwood fires, I held myself each day to a brief discipline of refeeling, reliving, and revising these poems. That enterprise taught me much about the process of revising poetry and the heightened level of honesty that revision demands. It also helped preserve my sanity in a difficult time, giving me a different and solitary clearing within which to recall the enduring qualities of the human spirit, and the girl and young woman I was when these poems were being written. I marveled at what she knew as well as what she did not know, and how she learned to put both together into a working poem.

I find these poems are still useful to me, and I wish to make them even more useful for other readers.

Audre Lorde
St. Croix, Virgin Islands
January 2, 1990–August 30, 1991

From COAL, FIRST CITIES,
and CABLES TO RAGE

part 1

MEMORIAL

If you come as softly
as wind within the trees
you may hear what I hear
see what sorrow sees.

If you come as lightly
as the threading dew
I will take you gladly
nor ask more of you.

You may sit beside me
silent as a breath
only those who stay dead
shall remember death.

If you come I will be silent
nor speak harsh words to you
I will not ask you why, now,
nor how, nor what you do.

But we shall sit here softly
beneath two different years
and the rich earth between us
shall drink our tears.

(1950)

MEMORIAL II

Genevieve
what are you seeing
in my mirror this morning
peering out like a hungry bird
behind my eyes
are you seeking the shape of a girl
I have grown less and less
to resemble
do you remember
I could not accept your face dying
do not know you now?

Surely your vision stayed
stronger than mine
Genevieve   tell me
where do dead girls wander
after their summer?

I wish I could see you again
far from me   even
birdlike   flying into the sun
your eyes are blinding me
Genevieve.

(1954)

RETURN

You did not clock the turning of the leaves
the silent browning of the grass
nor view brief bright November
rising out of the hills.

You came
with the sun set   the bough stripped
to the curtness of winter
an accomplished act.

So you well could say
"I never trusted autumn"
who did not cradle the weeping root
of flamed October sorrel
nor taste the bitter hard-won peace
red-browning autumn brought
one whom you loved
and left
to face the dark alone.

(1955)

TO A GIRL WHO KNEW
WHAT SIDE HER BREAD
WAS BUTTERED ON

He, through the eyes of the first marauder
saw her, his catch of bright thunder, heaping
tea and bread for her guardian dead
crunching the nut-dry words they said
and thinking the bones were sleeping
broke through the muffled afternoon
calling an end to their ritual's tune
with lightning-like disorder:

"Leave these bones, Love! Come away
from their summer breads with the flavor of hay
your guards can watch the shards of our catch
warming *our* bones on some winter's day!"

Like an ocean of straws the old bones rose
fearing the lightning's second death;
he had little time to wonder
at the silence of Bright Thunder
as, with a smile of pity and stealth,
she buttered fresh scones
for her guardian bones
as they trampled him into the earth.

(1955)

OAXACA

Beneath the carving drag of wood
the land moves slowly.
But lightning comes.

Growing their secret in brown earth
spread like a woman
daring
weary work for still-eyed men
who break the crust   nurse the seed
and a hard watch through the dry season.

Yet at the edge of bright thin day
past the split plow   they look
to the hills   to the brewing thunder
for the storm is known.

The land moves slowly.
Though the thunder's eye
can crack with a flash
the glass-brittle crust
of a mountain's face
the land moves slowly.

All a man's strength
his son's muscled arms
to carve one sleeve
into rock-defiant earth.
And the spread land waits.

Slow   long   the plowing
through dry-season brown
and the land moves slowly.

But lightning comes.

(1955)

GEMINI

Moon-minded the sun goes
farther from us
split into swirled days
smoky and unkempt
no longer young.

All the earth falls down
like lost light frightened
out between my fingers.

Here at the end of night
our love is a burnt-out ocean
a dry-worded, brittle bed.
Our roots, once nourished
by the cool lost water
cry out "Remind us!"
and the oyster world
cries out its pearls like tears.

Was this the wild calling
I heard in the long night past
wrapped in a stone-closed house?
I wakened to moon
to the sound-breached dark
and thinking a new word spoken
some promise made
broke through the screaming night
seeking a gateway out

But the night was dark
and love was a burning fence
about my house.

(1956)

PIROUETTE

I saw   your hands
on my lips   blind needles
blunted   from sewing up stone
where are you from
                    you said
your hands
reading over my lips
for some road through uncertain night
for your feet to examine home
where are you from
                    you said
your hands
on my lips like thunder
promising rain

A land where all lovers are mute.

Why are you weeping
                        you said
your hands in my doorway
like rainbows
following rain
why are you weeping

I have come home.

(1957)

THE MAIDEN

Once I was immortal
beside an ocean
having the names of night
and the first men came
with a sledge of fire
driving the sun.

I was brought forth
in the moonpit of a virgin
condemned to light
to a dry world's endless mornings
sweeping the moon away
and wherever I fled
seeking some new road home
morning had fingered
the harrowing rivers
to nest in the dried-out sparkling bed
of my mother sea.

Time drove the moon
down to crescent
and they found me
mortal
beside a moon's crater
mouthing
the ocean names of night.

(1958)

ECHO

I hear myself
drought caught   pleading
a windy cause
dry as the earth without rain
crying love
in a tongue of false thunder
while my love waits
a seeded trap
in the door of my house
a mouth full of perfect teeth
sure of their strength upon bone
waits
to swallow me whole
and pass me
as echoes of shadowless laughter.

Quiet   love hangs
in the door of my house
a sheet of brick-caught silk
rent in the sun.

(1958)

SUSPENSION

We entered silence
before the clock struck

red wine into crystal
not quite
fallen
the air solidifies
around your mouth
once wind has sucked the curtains in
like fright against the evening wall
prepared for storm
the room exhales
your lips
unfold
within their sudden opening
I hear the clock begin
to speak   again.

I remember now
the filled crystal   shattered
the wind-whipped curtains
bound
and the chill storm
finally broken
how the room felt
when your word was spoken

Warm
as the center of your palm
and as unfree.

(1959)

FATHER SON AND HOLY GHOST

I have not ever seen my father's grave.

Not that his judgment eyes
have been forgotten
nor his great hands' print
on our evening doorknobs
        one half turn each night
        and he would come
        drabbled with the world's business
        massive and silent
        as the whole day's wish
        ready to redefine
        each of our shapes
but now the evening doorknobs
wait   and do not recognize us
as we pass.

Each week a different woman
regular as his one quick glass
each evening
pulls up the grass his stillness grows
calling it weed.
Each week   a different woman
has my mother's face

and he
who time has   changeless
must be amazed
who knew and loved
but one.

My father died in silence
loving creation
and well-defined response
he lived   still judgments
on familiar things
and died   knowing
a January 15th that year me.

Lest I go into dust
I have not ever seen my father's grave.

(1960)

FATHER, THE YEAR
HAS FALLEN

Father   the year has fallen
leaves bedeck my careful flesh
like stone
one shard of brilliant summer
pierced me
and remains.
By this only   unregenerate bone
I am not dead
but waiting.

When the last warmth is gone
I shall bear in
the snow.

(1961)

BLOODBIRTH

That which is inside me
screaming
beating about for exit or entry
names the wind
wanting wind's power
wanting wind's voice
it is not my heart
and I am trying to speak
without art or embellishment
with bits of me flying out in all directions
screams   memories   old pieces of pain
struck off like dry bark
from a felled tree   bearing
up or out   holding or bringing forth
child or demon

Is this birth   or exorcism
or the beginning machineries of self
outlining   recalling
my father's business
what I must be about
my own business
minding.

Shall I split   or be cut down
by a word's complexion
or its lack
and from what direction
will the opening be made

to show the true face of me
lying exposed   and together

My children   your children
their children
all bent
on our conjugating business.

(1961)

COAL

I   is the total black
being spoken
from the earth's inside.

There are many kinds of open
how a diamond comes
into a knot of flame
how sound comes into a word
colored
by who pays what for speaking.

Some words are open
diamonds on a glass window
singing out within the crash
of passing sun
other words are stapled wagers
in a perforated book
buy and sign and tear apart
and come whatever wills all chances
the stub remains
an ill-pulled tooth
with a ragged edge.

Some words live in my throat
breeding like adders
others
know sun
seeking like gypsies
over my tongue

to explode through my lips
like young sparrows
bursting from shell.

Some words
bedevil me.

Love is a word, another kind of open.
As the diamond comes
into a knot of flame
I am Black
because I come from the earth's inside
take my word for jewel
in the open light.

(1962)

SONG

Wild trees have bought me
and will sell you a wind
in the forest of falsehoods
where your search must not end

for their roots are not wise.
Strip our loving of dream
pay its secrets to thunder
and ransom me home.

Beware oaks in laughter
know hemlock is lying
when she sings of defiance.
The sand words she's saying

will sift out and bury us
while the pale moons I hate
seduce you in phases
through oceans of light.

And the wild trees will sell me
for their safety from lightning
to sand that will flay me
for the next evening's planting.

They shall fill my limp skin
with wild dreams from their root
and grow from my dark flesh
new handfuls of hate

till our ransom is wasted
and the morning speaks out
in a thin voice of wisdom
that loves me too late.

(1962)

CONVERSATION IN CRISIS

I speak to you as a friend speaks
or a true lover
not out of friendship   or love
but for a clear meeting
of self upon self
in sight of our hearth
but without fire.

I cherish your words that ring
like late summer thunders
to sing without octave
and fade, having spoken the season.
But I hear the false heat of this voice
as it dries up the sides of your words
coaxing melodies from your tongue
and this curled music is treason.

Must I die in your fever
as the flames wax   take cover
in your heart's culverts
crouched like a stranger
under the scorched leaves
of your other burnt loves
until the storm passes over?

(1962)

NOW THAT I AM
FOREVER WITH CHILD

How the days went
while you were blooming within me
I remember   each upon each
the swelling changed planes of my body

how you first fluttered   then jumped
and I thought it was my heart.

How the days wound down
and the turning of winter
I recall   you
growing heavy against the wind.
I thought   now her hands
are formed   her hair
has started to curl
now her teeth are done
now she sneezes.

Then the seed opened.
I bore you one morning
just before spring
my head rang like a fiery piston
my legs were towers between which
a new world was passing.

Since then
I can only distinguish
one thread within running hours
you   flowing through selves
toward You.

(1963)

WHAT MY CHILD
LEARNS OF THE SEA

What my child learns of the sea
of the summer thunder
of riddles
that hide in the vortex of spring
she will learn in my twilight
and childlike
revise every autumn.

What my child learns
as her winters grow into time
has ripened in my own body
to enter her eyes
with first light.

This is why
more than blood
or the milk I have given
one day a strange girl
will step to the back
of a mirror
cutting my ropes
of sea   thunder   sun.

Of the ways
she will taste her autumns
toast-brittle or warmer than sleep
and the words
she will use for winter
I stand already condemned.

(1963)

THE WOMAN THING

The hunters are back
from beating the winter's face
in search of a challenge or task
in search of food
making fresh tracks
for their children's hunger
they do not watch the sun
they cannot wear its heat
for a sign of triumph
or freedom.

The hunters are treading heavily
homeward through snow
marked by their own bloody footprints.
Emptyhanded   the hunters return
snow-maddened
sustained by their rages.

In the night after food they will seek
young girls for their amusement.
Now the hunters are coming
and the unbaked girls
flee from their angers.

All this day I have craved
food for my child's hunger
emptyhanded
the hunters come shouting
injustice drips from their mouths
like stale snow
melted in sunlight.

The woman thing
my mother taught me
bakes off its covering of snow
like a rising Blackening sun.

(1964)

AND WHAT ABOUT
THE CHILDREN

We've made a child.
Now the dire predictions
have turned into wild   grim
speculations.
Still the negatives
are waiting   watching
and the relatives
keep
    right
        on
touching . . .
          and how much curl
          is right for a girl?

But if it is said
at some future date
that my son's head
is on
straight
he won't care
about his hair
nor give a damn
whose wife
I am.

(1964)

SUFFER THE CHILDREN

To Addie Mae Collins, 8, and Cynthia Wesley, 10, two
of four children killed in a racial bombing of a Baptist
church in Birmingham, Alabama, Sunday, September
16, 1963.

He is forever trapped
who suffers his own waste.
Rain leaching the earth   for lack
of roots to hold it
and children who are murdered
before their lives begin.

Who pays his crops to the sun
when his fields lie parched by drought
will mourn the lost water
waiting another rain.
But who shall disinter these girls
to love the women they were to become
or read the legends written beneath their skin?

We who love them remember their child's laughter.
But he whose hate robs him of their gold
has yet to weep at night above their graves.

A year rolls out.   Rains come again.
But however many girls be brought to sun
someday a man will thirst for sleep
in a southern night
seeking his peace where no peace is
and come to mourn these children
given to the dust.

(1964)

SPRING PEOPLE

FOR JONNO.

What anger in my hard-won bones
what heritage of water
makes me reject this insane season
fear to walk the earth
in spring?

At April and evening
I recall how we came
like new thunder
beating the earth
leaving the taste of rain and sunset
all our young hungers
before us.

Away from peaceful half-truths
and springtime passing unsaid
we came in the touch of fire
came to the sun
lay with the wild earth
until spent and knowing
we brought forth young.

Now insolent Aprils bedevil us
earthly conceits
reminding us
all else is forfeit
and only the blood-hungry children
remember
what face we had
what startling eyes.

(1965)

GENERATION

How the young attempt
and are broken
differs from age to age
we were brown free girls
love singing beneath our skin
sun in our hair   in our eyes
sun our fortune
and the wind had made us golden
made us gay.

In seasons of limitation
we wept out our promises
now these are the children we try
for temptations that wear our face.

But who comes back
from the latched cities of falsehood
warning
the road to nowhere
is slippery with our blood
warning
you need not drink the river
to get home
we have purchased bridges
with our mothers' bloody gold
now we are more than kin
who have come to share
not only blood
but the bloodiness of failure.

How the young are tempted
and betrayed
into slaughter or conformity
is a turn of the mirror
time's question only.

(1966)

BRIDGE THROUGH
MY WINDOW

In-curve scooped out and necklaced with light
burst pearls stream down
my outstretched arms to earth.
Oh bridge my sister bless me
before I sleep
the wild air is lengthening
and I am tried
beyond strength or bearing
over water.

Love, we are both shorelines
a left country   where time suffices
and the right land
where pearls roll into earth
and spring up day.
Joined
our bodies make a passage
without merging
as this slim necklace
is anchored into night.

And while the we conspires
to make secret its two eyes
we search the other shore
for some crossing home.

(1966)

A FAMILY RESEMBLANCE

My sister has my hair   my mouth   my eyes
and I presume her   trustless.
When she was young   open to any fever
wearing gold like a veil of fortune on her face
she waited through each rain
a dream of light.

But the sun came up
burning our eyes like crystal
bleaching the sky of promise and
my sister stood
Black   unblessed and unbelieving
shivering in the first cold show
of love.

I saw her gold become an arch
where nightmare hunted
the porches of her restless nights.
Through echoes of denial
she walks
a bleached side of reason
secret now
my sister never waits
nor mourns the gold
that wandered from her bed.

My sister has my tongue
and all my flesh
unanswered
and I presume her
trustless
as a stone.

(1966)

SUMMER ORACLE

Without expectation
there is no end
to the shock of morning
or even a small summer.

The image is fire
blackening the vague lines
into defiance
across this city.
The image is fire
sun warming us in a cold country
barren of symbols for love.

Now I have forsaken order
and imagine you into fire
untouchable in a magician's cloak
covered with symbols for destruction
and birth
sewn with griffins   hammers   arrows
gold sixes stitched into your hem
your fingers draw fire
but still the old warlocks shun you
for no gourds ring in your sack
no spells bring forth peace
and I am still fruitless and hungry
this summer
the peaches are flinty and juiceless
and cry sour worms.

The image is Fire
flaming over you   burning off excess
like the blaze planters start
to burn off bagasse from the canefields
before a harvest.

The image is fire
the high sign
ruling our summer
I smell it in the charred breeze
blowing over your body
close   hard   essential
under its cloak of lies.

(1967)

RITES OF PASSAGE

To MLK Jr.

Rock the boat to a fare-thee-well.
Once we suffered   dreaming
into the place where the children are playing
their child's games
where the children are hoping
knowledge survives if
unknowing
they follow the game
without winning.

Their fathers are dying
back to the freedom of wise children
playing
at knowing
their fathers are dying
whose deaths will not free them
from growing
from knowing
when the game becomes foolish
a dangerous pleading
for time out of power.

Quick   children
kiss us
we are growing
through dream.

(1968)

ROOMING HOUSES
ARE OLD WOMEN

Rooming houses are old women
rocking dark windows into their whens
waiting   incomplete circles___
rocking
rent office to stoop to
community bathrooms to gas-rings to
under-bed boxes of once useful garbage
city-issued with a twice-a-month check

and the young men next door
with their loud fragrant parties
and fishy rings left in the bathtub
no longer arouse them
from midnight to mealtime
no stops in between
light breaking
to pass through jumbled-up windows
and who was it who married that widow
that Buzzie's son messed with?

To Welfare and insult
from the slow shuffle
from dayswork to shopping bags
heavy with leftovers

Rooming houses
are old women waiting
searching

through darkening windows
the end or beginning of agony
old women seen through half-ajar doors
hoping   they are not waiting
but being
an entrance to somewhere
unknown   desired
but not new.

(1968)

ON A NIGHT OF THE FULL MOON

I

Out of my flesh that hungers
and my mouth that knows
comes the shape I am seeking
for reason.
The curve of your waiting body
fits my waiting hand
your breasts warm as sunlight
your lips quick as young birds
between your thighs the sweet
sharp taste of limes.

Thus I hold you
frank in my heart's eye
in my skin's knowing
as my fingers conceive your warmth
I feel your stomach
move against mine.

Before the moon wanes again
we shall come together.

II

And I would be the moon
spoken over your beckoning flesh
breaking against reservations
beaching thought

my hands at your high tide
over and under inside you
and the passing of hungers
attended   forgotten.

Darkly risen
the moon speaks
my eyes
judging   your roundness
delightful.

(1968)

HARD LOVE ROCK

I heard my heart screeching like a subway train
loudly enough to remind me it was still human
loudly enough to hurt   but telling me still
you were a ghost I had
better left in the cradle
telling me still
our tracks ran around
instead of straight out past the sewers
and I would have nothing for barter left
not even the print of love's grain
pressed into my flesh
from our wooden cross
splintered and shapeless
after the slaughter.

And when it was over
only pain.

(1968)

WHEN THE SAINTS
COME MARCHING IN

Plentiful sacrifice and believers in redemption
are all that is needed
so any day now I expect
some new religion
to rise up like tear gas
from the streets of New York
erupting like the rank pavement smell
released by a garbage truck's
baptismal drizzle.

High priests are ready and waiting
their incense pans full of fire.

I do not know their rituals
nor what name of the god
the survivors will worship
I only know she will be terrible
and very busy
and very old.

(1968)

DREAMS BITE

I

Dreams bite
Dreamer and legend
arm
at the edge of purpose
waking
I see the people of winter
put off their masks
to stain the earth red with blood
and on the outer edges of sleep
the people of sun
are carving their own children
into monuments
of war.

II

When I am absolute
at once
with the black earth
fire
I make my now

and power is spoken
peace
and hungry means never
or alone

I shall love
again

when I am obsolete.

(1968)

THE DOZENS

Nothing says that you must
see me in the street
with us so close together at that red light
a blind man could have smelled his grocer—
and nothing says that you must
say hello
as we pass in the street
but we have known each other
too well in the dark
for this
and it hurts me when you do not speak.

But no one you were with was quite so fine
that I won't remember this and
suffer you in turn and
in my own fashion which is
certainly not
in the street.

For I can count on my telephone
ringing some soft evening and you
exploding into my room
through the receiver
kissing and licking my ear. . . .

I hope you will learn your thing
at least
from some of those spiteful noseless people
who surround you
before the centipede in you
runs out of worlds

one for each foot.

(1968)

FANTASY AND
CONVERSATION

Speckled frogs leap from my mouth
drown in our coffee
between wisdoms
and decision.

I could smile
turn these frogs into pearls
speak of love
making and giving
if the spell works
shall I break down
or build what is broken
into a new house
shook with confusion

Shall I strike
before our magic
turns color?

(1968)

SOWING

It is the sink of the afternoon
the children asleep or weary
I have finished planting tomatoes
in brief sun   after four days of rain
brown earth under my fingernails
honey-thick sun on the back of my neck
the tips of my fingers are stinging
from the rich earth
but more so from the lack
of your body.

I have been to this place before
blood seething   commanded
my fingers fresh from the earth
dream of a furrow
whose name should be you.

(1968)

MARTHA

I

Martha   this is a catalog of days
passing before you looked again.
Someday you shall browse and order them
at will   or in your necessities.

I have taken a house at the Jersey shore
this summer. It is not my house.
Today the lightning bugs began.

On the first day you were dead.
With each breath your face
fell in like crumpled muslin.
We scraped together smashed images of flesh
preparing a memory. No words.
No words.

On the eighth day you startled the doctors
speaking from your death place
to reassure us you were still
trying.

Martha these are replacement days
should you ever need them
given
for those you once demanded
and never found.
May this trip be rewarding.

No one can fault you again Martha
for answering necessity too well.
May the gods who honor hard work
keep this second coming
free from that lack of choice
which hindered your first journey
to this Tarot house.

The doctors said
no hope   no dreaming
accept this case of flesh for evidence
of life without fire
wrapped you in an electric blanket
kept ten degrees below life.
Fetal hands curled inward
upon a bed so cold
bruises could not appear.

On the second day I knew you were alive
the gray flesh of your face
suffered.

I love you and cannot feel you less than Martha
I love you and cannot split this shaved head
from Martha's pushy straightness
asking   in a smash of mixed symbols
How long must I wander
in this final house of my father?

On the Solstice I was in Providence.
You know this town   we visited your friends here.
It rained in Providence on the Solstice
we passed through twice

on route 6 through Providence to the Cape
where we spent our second summer
trying for peace or equity.
It always seemed to be raining
by the time we got to Providence.
The Kirschenbaums live in Providence
and Blossom and Barry.
And Frances. And Frances.
Martha   I am in love again.

Listen, Frances, I said on the Solstice
our summer has started
today we are witches with enough energy
to move the mountain back.
Think of Martha.

Back in my hideous city
I saw you today. Your hair has grown
your armpits are scented
by some fastidious attendant.
testing   testing   testing
explosive syllables warning me
the mountain has fallen into dung
no Martha remember   remember Martha
warning   *dead flowers*
will not come to your bed again.

The sun has started south
our season is over.

Today you opened your eyes
they give
a blue-filmed history to your mangled words

´ help me understand how
you are teaching yourself to learn
again.

I *need you need me*
Je suis Martha I do not speak french kissing
OH WOW! Black and . . . Black and . . . beautiful?
Black and becoming
somebody else maybe Erica maybe
who sat in the fourth row
behind us in high school
but I never took French with you Martha
and who is this *Madame Erudite*
who is not me?

I found you today in a womb full of patients
blue-robed in various convalescences.
Your eyes are closed   you are propped
into a wheelchair, cornered, a parody of resting.
The bright glue of tragedy plasters all eyes
to a television set in the opposite corner
where a man is dying
step by step
in the american ritual going.
Someone has covered you
for this first public appearance
in a hospital gown, the badge of your next step.
Evocative voices flow from the set
horror is thick in this room
full of broken and mending receptions.

But no one has told you what it's all about   Martha
someone has shot another Kennedy

and we are drifting closer to what you predicted
your darkness is indeed speaking

Robert Kennedy is dying Martha
not you   not you   not you
he has a bullet in his brain Martha
But surgery was never considered for you
since there was no place to start
and no one intended to run you down on a highway
being driven home at 7:30 on a low summer evening
I gave a reading in Harlem that night
and who shall we try for this shaven head now
in the courts of heart Martha
where his murder is televised over and over
with residuals
they have caught the man who shot Robert Kennedy
another one of difficult journeys—
he has a bullet in his brain Martha
and much less of a chance than you.

On the first day of July you warned me again
the threads are broken
you darkened into explosive angers
refused to open your eyes, humming interference
your thoughts are not over Martha
they are you   their task is
to remember Martha
we can help with the other
the mechanics of blood and bone
and you cut through the pain of my words
to warn me again
testing testing whoever passes

must tear out their hearing aids
for the duration.

 I hear you explaining Neal
my husband whoever must give me a present
he has to give me
himself where I can find him for
where can he look at himself
in the mirror I am making
or over my bed where the window
is locked into battle with a wall?

Now I sit in New Jersey
with lightning bugs and mosquitoes
typing and thinking of you.
Tonight you started seizures
a temporary relapse
but this lake is far away Martha
and I sit unquiet in New Jersey
thinking of you.

I Ching the Book of Changes
says I am impertinent to ask of you obliquely
but I have no direct question
only need.
When I cast an oracle today
it spoke of the Abysmal again
very difficult but promising
in it water finds its own level, flowing
out from the lowest point.
I cast another one also that cautioned
the superior man to seek his strength
only in its own season.

Martha what did we learn from our brief season
when the summer grackles rang in my walls?
one and one is too late now
you journey through darkness alone
leafless I sit far from my present house
and the grackles' voices are dying

we shall love each other here if ever at all.

II

Yes foolish prejudice lies
I hear you Martha
that you would never harm my children
but you have forgotten their names
and that you are Elizabeth's godmother.
You offer me coral rings, watches
even your body
if I will help you sneak home.

No Martha my blood is not muddy   my hands
are not dirty to touch   Martha
I do not know your night nurse's name
even though she is Black
yes I did live in Brighton Beach once
which is almost Rockaway
one bitter winter
but not with your night nurse Martha
and yes I agree this is one hell
of a summer.

No you cannot walk yet Martha
and no the medicines you are given

to quiet your horrors
have not affected your brain
yes it is very hard to think but
it is getting easier   yes Martha
we have loved each other and yes I hope
we still can
no Martha I do not know if we shall ever
sleep in each other's arms again.

III

It is the middle of August and you are alive
to discomfort. You have been moved
into a utility room across the hall
from the critical ward because your screaming
disturbs the other patients
your bedside table has been moved also
which means you will be there for a while
a favorite now with the floor nurses
who put up a sign on the utility room door
I'M MARTHA HERE   DO NOT FORGET ME
PLEASE KNOCK.

A golden attendant named Sukie
bathes you as you proposition her
she is very pretty and very gentle.
The frontal lobe governs inhibitions
the damage is after all slight
and they say the screaming will pass.

Your daughter Dorrie promises you
will be as good as new, Mama
who only wants to be *Bad as the old.*

I want some truth good hard truth
a sign of youth
we were all young once we had
a good thing going
now I'm making a plan
for a dead rabbit a rare rabbit.
I am dying goddammit dying am I
Dying?
Death is a word you can say   now
pain is mortal
I am dying for god's sake won't someone please
get me a doctor PLEASE
your screams beat against our faces
you yell
begging relief from the blank cruelty
of a thousand nurses.
A moment of silence breaks
as you accumulate fresh sorrows
then through your pain-fired face
you slip me a wink.

Martha Winked.

IV

Your face straightens into impatience
with the loads of shit you are handed
'You're doing just fine Martha what time is it Martha'
'What did you have for supper tonight Martha'
testing testing whoever passes for Martha
you weary of it.

Those you must straighten out
pass your bedside in the utility room
bringing you cookies
and hoping
you will be kinder than they ever were.

Go away Mama and Bubie
for 30 years you made me believe
I was shit you shat out for the asking
but I'm not and you'd better believe it
right now would you kindly
stop rubbing my legs
and GET THE HELL OUT OF HERE.
Next week Bubie bring teglach
your old favorite
and will you be kinder Martha
that we were to the shell   the cocoon
out of which the you is emerging?

V

No one you were can come so close
to death without dying
into another Martha.
I await you
as we all await her
fearing her honesty
fearing
we may neither love nor dismiss
Martha with the dross burned away
fearing
condemnation from the essential.

You cannot get closer to death than this Martha
the nearest you've come to living yourself.

(June–August 1968)

POEM FOR A POET

I think of a coffin's quiet
when I sit in the world of my car
separate and observing
windows closed and washed clean
in rain. I like to sit and watch
other worlds pass. Yesterday evening
I sat in my car on Sheridan Square
flat and broke and a little bit damp
thinking about money and rain
and the Village broads with narrow hips
rolling like drunken shovels
down Christopher Street.

Then I saw you unmistakably
darting out from between a police car and
what used to be Atkin's all-night diner—
where we sat making bets the last time I saw you
on how many busts we could count
through the plate-glass window
in those last skinny hours before dawn
with our light worded-out but still burning
the earlier evening's promise
dregs in our coffee cups
and I saw you dash out and turn left at the corner
your beard spiky with rain and refusing
shelter under your chin.

But I had thought you were dead Jarrell
struck down by a car at sunset on a North Carolina road

or were you the driver
tricked into a fatal swerve by some twilit shadow
or was that Frank O'Hara
or Conrad Kent Rivers
and you
the lonely spook in a Windy City motel
draped in the secrets of your convulsive death
all alone   all poets   all loved
and dying alone   that final death
less real than those deaths you lived
and for which I forgave you?

I watched you hurry down Fourth Street Jarrell
from the world of my car in the rain
remembering Spring Festival Night
at Women's College in North Carolina
and wasn't that world a coffin's retreat
of spring whispers   romance   rhetoric
Untouched   by winds
buffeting up the road from Greensboro
and nobody mentioned the Black Revolution
or Sit-Ins   or Freedom Rides   or SNCC
or cattleprods in Jackson Mississippi—
where I was to find myself
how many years later:

You were mistaken that night and I told you
in a letter beginning   Dear Jarrell
if you sit in one place long enough
the whole world will pass you by . . .
you were wrong when you said I took
living too seriously
meaning   you were afraid

I might take you   too seriously
you shouldn't have worried
I dug you too much
to put you down
but I never took you at all
except as a good piece of my first journey south
except as I take you now
gladly   at a distance
and wondering   as I have so often
how come   being so cool
you weren't also a little bit
Black.

And also why have you returned
to this dying city
and what piece of me is it then
buried down there in North Carolina.

(1970)

STORY BOOKS ON
A KITCHEN TABLE

Out of her womb of pain my mother spat me
into her ill-fitting harness of despair
into her deceits
where anger reconceived me
piercing my eyes like arrows
pointed by her nightmare
of who I was not
becoming.

Going away
she left me in her place
iron maidens to protect me
and for my food
the wrinkled milk of legend
where I wandered
through lonely rooms of afternoon
wrapped in nightmare
from the Orange   Red   Yellow
Purple   Blue   Green
Fairy Books
where white witches ruled
over the kitchen table
and never wept
or offered gold
nor any kind enchantment
for the vanished mother
of a Black girl.

(1970)

From A LAND WHERE OTHER
PEOPLE LIVE

part 2

EQUINOX

My daughter marks the day that spring begins.
I cannot celebrate spring without remembering
how the bodies of unborn children
bake in their mothers' flesh like ovens
consecrated by the flame that eats them
lit by mobiloil and easternstandard
Unborn children in their blasted mothers
floating   monuments
in an ocean of oil.

The year my daughter was born
DuBois died in Accra while I
marched into Washington
to the death knell of dreaming
which 250,000 others mistook for a hope
believing only Birmingham's Black children
were being pounded into mortar in churches
that year   some of us still thought
Vietnam was a suburb of Korea.

Then John Kennedy fell off the roof
of Southeast Asia and shortly afterward
my whole house burned down
with nobody in it
and on the following Sunday
my borrowed radio announced
that Malcolm was shot dead
and I ran to reread all he had written
because death was becoming such an excellent measure

of prophecy
As I read his words   dark mangled children
came streaming out of the atlas
Hanoi   Angola   Guinea-Bissau   Mozambique   Phnom Penh
merging into Bedford-Stuyvesant and Hazelhurst Mississippi
haunting my New York tenement that terribly bright summer
while Detroit and Watts and San Francisco were burning
I lay awake in stifling Broadway nights   afraid
for whoever was growing in my belly
and suppose it started earlier than planned
who would I trust to take care that my daughter
did not eat poisoned roaches
when I was gone?

If she did, it doesn't matter
because I never knew it.
Today both children came home from school
talking about spring and peace
and I wonder if they will ever know it
I want to tell them that we have no right to spring
because our sisters and brothers are burning
because every year the oil grows thicker
and even the earth is crying
because Black is beautiful but currently
going out of style
that we must be very strong
and love each other
in order to go on living.

(1969)

THE SEVENTH
SENSE

Women
who build nations
learn
to love
men
who build nations
learn
to love
children
building sand castles
by the rising sea.

(1969)

CHANGE OF SEASON

Am I to be cursed forever with becoming
somebody else on the way to myself?

Walking backwards I fall into summers
behind me   salt with wanting
lovers or friends   a job   wider shoes
a cool drink   something to bite into   freshness
a place to hide out of the rain
out of the shifting melange of seasons
where cruel boys i chased
and their skinny dodgeball sisters
flamed and died in becoming
the brown autumn
left in search of who tore the streamers down
at graduation   christmas   my wedding day
and as winter wore out the babies came
angry effort and reward
in their appointed seasons
my babies tore out of me
like poems   after
I slept and woke
promise had come again
this time more sure than the dream of being
sweet sixteen and somebody else
walking five miles through the august city
with a free dog   hoping
now we could be the allamerican family

we had just gotten a telephone
and the next day my sister cut his leash
on Broadway

That dog of my childhood bays at the new moon
as I reach into time up to my elbows
extracting the taste and sharp smell
of my first lover's neck
rough as the skin of a brown pear ripening
I was so terribly sure
I would come forever to April
with my first love who died on a Sunday morning
poisoned and wondering
was summer ever coming.

As I face the ocean of seasons
they separate
into distinct and particular faces
listening to a cover begin to crack open
whether or not the fruit is worth waiting
thistles and arrows and apples are blooming
individual beautiful faces   smiling   moving
even the pavement begins to flow
into new concretions
the eighth day is coming

I have paid dearly in time for love
I hoarded   unseen
summer goes into my words
and comes out reason.

(1969)

FOR EACH OF YOU

Be who you are and will be
learn to cherish
that boisterous Black Angel that drives you
up one day and down another
protecting the place where your power rises
running like hot blood
from the same source
as your pain.

When you are hungry
learn to eat
whatever sustains you
until morning
but do not be misled by details
simply because you live them.

Do not let your head deny
your hands
any memory of what passes through them
nor your eyes   nor your heart
everything can be used
except what is wasteful
(you will need to remember this
when you are accused of destruction).
Even when they are dangerous
examine the heart of those machines
which you hate
before you discard them
but do not mourn their lack of power

lest you be condemned
to relive them.

If you do not learn to hate
you will never be lonely
enough   to love easily
nor will you always be brave
although it does not grow any easier.

Do not pretend to convenient beliefs
even when they are righteous
you will never be able to defend your city
while shouting

Remember   our sun
is not the most noteworthy star
only the nearest.

Respect whatever pain you bring back
from your dreaming
but do not look for new gods
in the sea
nor in any part of a rainbow.

Each time you love
love as deeply
as if it were
forever
only nothing is
eternal.

Speak proudly to your children
where ever you may find them
tell them
you are the offspring of slaves
and your mother was
a princess
in darkness.

(1970)

NEW YEAR'S DAY

This day feels put together hastily
like a gift for grateful beggars
being better than no time at all
but bells are ringing
in cities I have never visited
and my name is printed over doorways
I have never seen.

Extracting a bone
or whatever is tender or fruitful
from a core of indifferent days
I have forgotten the touch of sun
cutting through uncommitted mornings
The night is full of messages
I cannot read
I am too busy forgetting
air like fur on my tongue
these tears
do not come from sadness
but from grit in the sometimes wind.

Rain falls like tar on my skin
my son picks up a chicken heart at dinner
asking   "Does this thing love?"

Ghostly unmalicious fingers
pluck over my dreaming
hiding whatever it is of sorrow
that would profit me
I am deliberate
and afraid
of nothing.

(1970)

GOOD MIRRORS ARE
NOT CHEAP

It is a waste of time to hate a mirror
or its reflection
instead of stopping the hand
that makes glass with distortions
slight enough to pass
unnoticed
until one day peering
into your face
under a merciless light
the fault in a mirror slaps back
becoming what you think
is the shape of your error
and if I am beside that self
you destroy me
or if you can see
the mirror is lying
you shatter the glass
choosing another blindness
slashed helpless hands.

At the same time
down the street
a glassmaker is grinning
turning out new mirrors
that lie . . .
selling us new clowns
at cut rate.

(1970)

AS I GROW UP AGAIN

A little boy wears my mistakes
like a favorite pair of shorts
outgrown   at six
my favorite excuse was morning
and I remember that I hated
spring's change.

At play within my childhood
my son works hard   learning
which doors do not open easily
and which clocks will not work
he toys with anger like a young cat
testing its edges
slashing through the discarded box
where I laid my childish dreams to rest
and brought him brown and wriggling
to his own house.

He learns there through my error
winning with secrets
I do not need to know.

(1970)

NEIGHBORS

For D.D.

We made strong poems for each other
exchanging formulas for each particular magic
all the time pretending
we were not really witches
and each time we would miss
some small ingredient
that one last detail
that could make the spell work
Each one of us   too busy
hearing the other voices
the sound of our own guards
calling the watch at midnight
assuring us
we were still safe and asleep
so when it came time to practice
what we had learned
one grain was always missing
one word unsaid
and the pot did not boil
the sweet milk would curdle
or the bright wound went on bleeding
and each of us went back
to her own particular magic

confirmed   believing
she was always alone
believing
the other
was always lying
in wait.

(1970)

LOVE, MAYBE

Always
in the middle
of our bloodiest battles
you lay down your arms
like flowering mines

to conqueror me home.

(1970)

CONCLUSION

Passing men in the street who are dead
becomes a common occurrence
but loving one of them
is no solution.
I believe in love as I believe in our children
but I was born Black and without illusion
and my vision
which differs from yours
is clear
although sometimes restricted.

I have watched you at midnight
moving through casual sleep
wishing I could afford the nondesperate dreams
that stir you   to wither and fade
into partial solutions.
Your nights are wintery long and very young
full of purity and forgiveness
and a meek Jesus who rides through your cities
on a barren ass whose braying
does not include a future tense.

But I wear my nights as I wear my life
and my dying
absolute and unforgiven
nuggets of compromise and decision
fossilized by fierce midsummer sun
and when I dream

I move through a Black land
where the future
glows eternal and green
but where the symbols for now
are bloody and unrelenting
rooms
where confused children
with wooden stumps for fingers
play at war
and cannot pick up their marbles
or run away home
whenever a nightmare threatens.

(1970)

THE WINDS OF ORISHA

I

This land will not always be foreign.
How many of its women ache to bear their stories
robust and screaming like the earth erupting grain
or thrash in padded chains mute as bottles
hands fluttering traces of resistance
on the backs of once lovers
half the truth
knocking in the brain like an angry steampipe
how many   long to work or split open
so bodies venting into silence
can plan the next move?

Tiresias took 500 years they say
to progress into woman
growing smaller and darker and more powerful
until nut-like, she went to sleep in a bottle
Tiresias took 500 years to grow into woman
so do not despair of your sons.

II

Impatient legends speak through my flesh
changing this earth's formation
spreading
I become myself   an incantation
dark raucous characters
leaping back and forth across bland pages
Mother Yemanja raises her breasts to begin my labor
near water
the beautiful Oshun and I lie down together
in the heat of her body's truth
my voice comes stronger
Shango will be my brother roaring out of the sea
earth shakes our darkness
swelling into each other
warning winds announce us living
as Oya, Oya my sister my daughter
destroys the crust of the tidy beaches
and Eshu's Black laughter
turns up the neat sleeping sand.

III

The heart of this country's tradition is its wheat men
dying for money
dying for water   for markets   for power
over all people's children
they sit in their chains on their dry earth
before nightfall
telling tales as they wait for completion
hoping the young ones can hear them
earthshaking fear wreathes their blank weary faces
most of them have spent their lives and their wives
in labor
most of them have never seen beaches
but as Oya my sister moves out of the mouths
of their sons and daughters against them
I swell up from the page of their daily heralds
leap out of the almanacs
instead of an answer to their search for rain
they will read me
the dark cloud
meaning something entire
and different.

When the winds of Orisha blow
even the roots of grass
quicken.

(1970)

WHO SAID IT WAS
SIMPLE

There are so many roots to the tree of anger
that sometimes the branches shatter
before they bear.

Sitting in Nedicks
the women rally before they march
discussing the problematic girls
they hire to make them free.
An almost white counterman passes
a waiting brother to serve them first
and the ladies neither notice nor reject
the slighter pleasures of their slavery.

But I who am bound by my mirror
as well as my bed
see cause in color
as well as sex.

and sit here wondering
which me will survive
all these liberations.

(1970)

THE DAY THEY
EULOGIZED MAHALIA

The day they eulogized Mahalia
the echoes of her big voice stilled
and the mourners found her
singing out from their sisters' mouths
from their mothers' toughness
from the funky dust in the corners
of Sunday church pews
sweet and dry and simple
and that hated Sunday morning fussed-over feeling
the songs
singing out from their mothers' toughness
would never threaten the lord's retribution
anymore.

Now she was safe
acceptable   that big Mahalia
Chicago turned all out
to show her that they cared
but her eyes were closed
And although Mahalia loved our music
nobody sang her favorite song
and while we talked about
what a hard life she had known
and wasn't it too bad Sister Mahalia
didn't have it easier   earlier
SIX BLACK CHILDREN
BURNED TO DEATH IN A DAY CARE CENTER
on the South Side

kept in a condemned house
for lack of funds
firemen found their bodies
like huddled lumps of charcoal
with silent mouths wide open.

Small and without song
six Black children found a voice in flame
the day the city eulogized Mahalia.

(1971)

PROGRESS REPORT

When you do say hello I am never sure
if you are being saucy or experimental or
merely protecting some new position.
Sometimes you gurgle while asleep
and I know tender places still intrigue you.
When you question me on love now
shall I recommend a dictionary
or myself?

You are the child of wind and ravens I created
always my daughter   I cannot recognize
the currents where you swim and dart
through my loving
upstream to your final place of birth
but you never tire of hearing
how I crept out of my mother's house
at dawn, with an olive suitcase
crammed with books and fraudulent letters
and an unplayed guitar.

I see myself flash through your eyes
in moments   caught between history
and obedience
those moments grow each day
before you comply
as, when did washing dishes
change from privilege to chore?
I watch the hollows deepen over your hips
wondering if I have taught you Black enough

until I see
all kinds of loving still intrigue
you   growing more and more
dark rude and tender
unafraid.

What you once took for granted
you now refuse to take at all
even I   knock before I enter
the shoals of furious choices
not my own
that flood through your secret reading
nightly   under cover.

I have not yet seen you, but
I hear the pages rustle
from behind closed doors.

(1971)

BLACK MOTHER WOMAN

I cannot recall you gentle
yet through your heavy love
I have become
an image of your once-delicate flesh
split with deceitful longings.

When strangers come and compliment me
your aged spirit takes a bow
jingling with pride
but once you hid that secret
in the center of your fury
hanging me
with deep breasts and wiry hair
your own split flesh
and long-suffering eyes
buried in myths of little worth.

But I have peeled away your anger
down to its core of love
and look mother
I am   a dark temple
where your true spirit rises
beautiful   tough as chestnut
stanchion against nightmares of weakness
and if my eyes conceal
a squadron of conflicting rebellions
I learned from you
to define myself
through your denials.

(1971)

TEACHER

I make my children promises
in wintery afternoons
lunchtime stories
when my feet hurt from talking too much
and not enough movement
except in my own
worn down at the heel shoes
except in little circles of broken-down light
I am trapped in
the intensities of my own (our) situation
where what we need and do not have
deadens us
and promises sound like destruction.

White snowflakes clog the passages
drifting through halls and corridors
while I tell stories with no ending
at lunchtime
the children's faces wear uneasy smiles
like a heavy question
food is provided with a frightening efficiency
the talk is free/dom meaning state
condition of being.

We are elementary forces
colliding in free fall.

And who will say I made promises
better kept in confusion

than time   grown tall and straight
in a season of snow
in a harsh time of sun that withers
who will say as they build
ice castles at noon
living promises I made
these children   who will say
we have laid out the new cities
with more love than our dreams?

Who will hear   freedom's bell deaden
in the clang of the gates of the prisons
where snowmen melt into darkness
unforgiven and so remembered?

How we romped through so many winters
made snowballs   played at war. . . .

As the promises I make children
sprout like wheat from an early spring's wager
who will hear freedom
ring in the chains of promise
who will forget the curse
of the outsider
who will not recognize our season
as free
who will say
Promise corrupts
what it does not invent?

(1971)

GENERATION II

A Black girl   going
into the woman
her mother   desired
and prayed for
walks alone   afraid
of both their angers.

(1971)

RELEVANT IS DIFFERENT
POINTS ON THE CIRCLE

To BWC.

History   bless me
with my children's growing rebellion
with love in another tongue
teach me what my pride will not savor
like the fabled memory of elephants
I have loved them and watched over them
as the bird forgets but the trap doesn't
and I shall be buried with the bones of an eagle
with a fierce detachment
and legends of the slain buffalo.

This is a country where other people live.

When agate replaces dead wood
slowly opal and bone become one.
A phoenix named Angela
nests in my children's brain
already growing herds of bison
unnoticed   are being hunted down
the federal canyons of Yellowstone Park.

(1971)

DEAR TONI
INSTEAD OF A LETTER OF
CONGRATULATION UPON YOUR
BOOK AND YOUR DAUGHTER
WHOM YOU SAY YOU ARE
RAISING TO BE A CORRECT
LITTLE SISTER

I can see your daughter walking down streets of love
in revelation;
but raising her up to be a correct little sister
is doing your mama's job all over again.
And who did you make on the edge of Harlem's winter
hard and black
while the inside was undetermined
swirls of color and need
shifting, remembering
were you making another self to rediscover
in a new house and a new name
in a new place next to a river of blood
or were you putting the past together
pooling everything learned
into a new and continuous woman
divorced from the old shit we share
and shared and sharing need not share again?

I see your square delicate jawbone
the mark of a Taurus (or Leo) as well as the ease
with which you deal with pretensions.
I dig your going and becoming .

the lessons you teach your daughter
our history
for I am your sister corrected
already raised up
our daughters will explore the old countries
as curious visitors to our season
using their own myths to keep themselves sharp.

I have known you over and over again
as I've lived through this city
taking it in storm and morning strolls
through Astor Place and under the Canal Street Bridge
The Washington Arch a stone raised to despair
Riverside Drive too close to the dangerous predawn
waters and 129th Street
between Lenox and Seventh
burning my blood but not Black enough
and threatening to become home.

I first saw you behind a caseworker's notebook
defying upper Madison Avenue and my roommate's concern
the ghost of Maine lobsterpots trailing behind you
and I followed you into East Fourth Street and out
through Bellevue's side entrance one night
into the respectable vineyards of Yeshiva's intellectual gloom
and there I lost you between the books and the games
until I rose again out of Jackson Mississippi
to find you in an office down the hall from mine
calmly studying term papers like maps
marking off stations
on our trip through the heights of Convent Avenue
teaching English   our children   citycollege
softer and tougher and more direct

and putting your feet up on a desk you say Hi
I'm going to have a baby
so now I can really indulge myself.

Through that slim appraisal of your world
I felt you   grinning and plucky
and a little bit scared
perhaps of the madness past that had relieved you
through your brittle young will of iron
into the fire of whip steel.

I have a daughter also
who does not remind me of you
she too has deep aquatic eyes
that are burning and curious.
As she moves through taboos
whirling myth like a gay hoop over her head
I know beyond fear and history
that our teaching means keeping trust
with less and less correctness
only with ourselves
History may alter   old pretenses and victories
but not the pain   my sister   never the pain.

In my daughter's name
I bless your child with the mother she has
with a future of warriors and growing fire.
But with tenderness also
we are landscapes, Toni,
printed upon them as surely
as water etches feather on stone.

Our girls will grow into their own
Black Women
finding their own contradictions
they will come to love
as I love you.

(September 1971)

PROLOGUE

Haunted by poems beginning with I
seek out those whom I love who are deaf
to whatever does not destroy
or curse the old ways that did not serve us
while history falters and our poets are dying
choked into silence by icy distinction
death rattles blind curses
and I hear even my own voice becoming
a pale strident whisper
At night sleep locks me into an echoless coffin
sometimes at noon I dream
there is nothing to fear
now standing up in the light of my father sun
without shadow
I speak without concern for the accusations
that I am too much or too little woman
that I am too Black or too white
or too much myself
and through my lips come the voices
of the ghosts of our ancestors
living and moving among us.

Hear my heart's voice as it darkens
pulling old rhythms out of the earth
that will receive this piece of me
and a piece of each one of you
when our part in history quickens again
and is over:

Hear
the old ways are going away
and coming back pretending change
masked as denunciation and lament
masked as a choice
between an eager mirror that blurs and distorts us
in easy definitions   until our image
shatters along its fault
or the other half of that choice
speaking to our hidden fears with a promise
our eyes need not seek any truer shape—
a face at high noon particular and unadorned—
for we have learned to fear
the light from clear water might destroy us
with reflected emptiness or a face without tongue
with no love or with terrible penalties
for any difference
and even as I speak remembered pain is moving
shadows over my face, my own voice fades and
my brothers and sisters are leaving;

Yet when I was a child
whatever my mother thought would mean survival
made her try to beat me whiter every day
and even now the color of her bleached ambition
still forks throughout my words
but I survived
and didn't I survive   confirmed
to teach my children where her errors lay
etched across their faces between the kisses
that she pinned me with asleep
and my mother beating me
as white as snow melts in the sunlight

loving me into her bloods black bone—
the home of all her secret hopes and fears
and my dead father whose great hands
weakened in my judgment
whose image broke inside of me
beneath the weight of failure
helps me to know who I am not
weak or mistaken
my father loved me alive
to grow and hate him
and now his grave voice joins hers
within my words   rising and falling
are my sisters and brothers listening?

The children remain
like blades of grass over the earth and
all the children are singing
louder than mourning
all their different voices
sound like a raucous question
they do not fear empty mirrors
they have seen their faces defined in a hydrant's puddle
before the rainbows of oil obscured them.
The time of lamentation and curses is passing.

My mother survives
through more than chance or token.
Although she will read what I write
with embarrassment   or anger
and a small understanding
my children do not need to relive my past
in strength nor in confusion
nor care that their holy fires

may destroy
more than my failures.

Somewhere in the landscape past noon
I shall leave a dark print of the me that I am
and who I am not
etched in a shadow
of angry and remembered loving
and their ghosts will move
whispering through them
with me none the wiser
for they will have buried me
either in shame
or in peace.

And the grasses will still be
Singing.

(November 1971)

MOVING OUT OR THE END OF
COOPERATIVE LIVING

For Cuz Gerry.

I am so glad to be moving
away from this prison for Black and white faces
assaulting each other with our joint oppression
competing for who pays the highest price for this privilege
I am so glad I am moving
technicolored complaints aimed at my head
mash up on my door like mosquitoes
each time my lips move sideways
the smile shatters on the in-thing racing
dictator through our hallways
on concrete faces   on soul compactors
on the rhetoric of incinerators and plastic drapes
for the boiler room
on legends of broken elevators
blowing my morning cool
avoiding me in the corridors
dropping their load on my face down 24 stories
of lives in a spectrumed madhouse
pavilion of gnats and nightmare remembering
once we all saved like beggars
to buy our way into this castle
of fantasy and forever now
I am so glad to be moving.

Last month a tenant was asked to leave
someone saw him wandering
one morning up and down the tenth floor

with no clothes on
having locked himself out the night before
with the garbage
he could not fit into the incinerator
but it made no difference
the Floor Captain cut the leads to his cable TV
he left covered in tangled wires of shame
his apartment was reconsecrated by an exterminator
I am so glad I am moving.

Although workmen will descend at $100 an hour
to scrape my breath from the walls
refinish the air and the floors with their eyes
and charge me the exact amount
of whatever is owed me
called equity
I am so glad to be moving
from the noise of psychic footsteps
beating a tune that is not my own
louder than any other sound in the neighborhood
except the blasting that goes on all day and all night
from the city's new toilet being built
outside our main entrance
from the spirits who live in the locks
of the other seven doors
bellowing secrets of living hells revealed
but not shared
for everybody's midnights
know what the walls hide
our toilets are made of glass
wired for sound

24 stories
full of tears flushing at midnight
our only community room
children set their clocks to listen at the tissue walls
gazing upward from their stools
from one flight to another
catching the neighbors in private struggle
next morning it will all be discussed
at length in the elevators
with no secrets left
I am so glad to be moving
no more dreams of caged puppies
grinding their teeth into cartoon-like faces
that half-plead   half-snicker
then fold under and vanish
back into snarling strangers
I am so glad I am moving.

But when this grim house goes
slipping into the sewer prepared for it
this whole city can read
its own obituary
written on the broken record of dreams
of ordinary people
who wanted what they could not get
and so pretended to be someone else.

Ordinary people having
what they never learned to want
themselves
and so becoming pretension
concretized.

(1972)

SIGNS

No one is left to eat by my fire.
My children have gone to the wood
their earth-colored laughter
stitched up in a market blanket
I wore to announce my coming of age
and that day
other girls went pale and wanting
between the stalls in the noon sun.

May their journey be free from ghosts.
I have heard the old spirits chattering
down by the river   planning my downfall
for my yam has always been eaten
with pleasure
and my body has not been unfruitful
I do not squander my days at the market
nor bargain for what I cannot sell
I do not cover my yams with a cloth
when creditors pass
pretending they belong to another.

But I have only two children.
neither was born in conjure nor hiding
now they go to the wood
to the night   to the gradual breaking.
They will return   men
and silent
draped in impatience and indigo
signs of our separation.

As I go to wash myself before sun
I search my dooryard and tremble
lest I find the shattered pot
left as a sign to warn me
they will never return.

(1972)

MOVEMENT SONG

I have studied the tight curls
on the back of your neck
moving away from me   beyond anger
or failure   your face
in the evening schools of longing
through mornings of wish and ripen
we were always saying goodbye
in the blood   in the bone   over coffee
before dashing for elevators   going
in opposite directions
without goodbyes.

Do not remember me as a bridge   nor a roof
as the maker of legends   nor as a trap
door to the world
where Black and white clericals
hang on the edge of beauty
in five o'clock elevators
twitching their shoulders
to avoid other flesh
and now
there is someone to speak for them
moving away from me   into tomorrows
morning of wish and ripen
your goodbye is a promise of lightning
in the last angel's hand
unwelcome   warning
the sands have run out against us
we were rewarded by journeys

away from each other   into desire
into mornings alone
where excuse and endurance mingle
conceiving decision.

Do not remember me
as disaster
nor as the keeper of secrets
I am a fellow rider in the cattle cars
watching   you move   slowly
out of my bed
saying we cannot waste time
only ourselves.

(1972)

From NEW YORK HEAD
SHOP AND MUSEUM

part 3

MENTOR

Scaling your words like crags I found
silence   speaking
in a mouthful of sun
yet I say you are young
for your lips are not stone
to the rain's fall
I say you are lovely to speak
in a mouthful of sun
nor does summer await you.

I see the midnight
heavy as windows sealed against fire
and tears coiled like snakes
in your eyes
I see your forehead like snow
and the names of so many winters
your fingers play over
plucking out rays of light
to anoint me home;

Yet I say you are young
and your lips are not stone
to be weathered
rather a song
learned when my aprils were fallow.
I sing this for beacon
lighting us home
each to our separate house.

(1959)

REVOLUTION
IS ONE FORM
OF SOCIAL
CHANGE

When the man is busy
making niggers
it doesn't matter
whose shade
you are.

If he runs out of one
particular color
he can always switch
to size
and when he's finished
off the big ones
he'll change to sex
which is   after all
where it all began.

(1968)

THE AMERICAN CANCER
SOCIETY OR THERE IS MORE
THAN ONE WAY TO SKIN A COON

Of all the ways in which this country
Prints its death upon me
Selling me cigarettes is one of the most certain
Yet every day I watch my son digging
ConEdison GeneralMotors GarbageDisposal
Out of his nose as he watches a 3-second spot
On How To Stop Smoking
And it makes me sick to my stomach.
It is not by cigarettes
That you intend to destroy my children.

Not even by the cold white light of moon-walks
While half the boys I knew
Are doomed by quicker trips in a different capsule;
No, the american cancer destroys
By seductive and reluctant admission
For instance
Black women no longer give birth through our ears
and therefore have A Monthly Need For Iron:
For instance
Our Pearly teeth are *not* racially insured
And therefore must be Gleemed For Fewer Cavities:
For instance
Even though the astronauts are white
Perhaps Black People *can* develop
Some human attributes
Requiring

Dried dog food frozen coffee instant oatmeal
Depilatories deodorants detergents
And other assorted plastic.

This is the surest sign I know
The american cancer society is dying—
It has started to dump its symbols onto Black People
A convincing proof those symbols are now useless
And far more lethal than emphysema.

(1969)

A SEWERPLANT GROWS IN HARLEM OR I'M A STRANGER HERE MYSELF WHEN DOES THE NEXT SWAN LEAVE

How is the word   made flesh   made steel   made shit
by ramming it into No Exit like a homemade bomb
until it explodes
smearing itself   made real
against our already filthy windows
or by flushing it down in a verbal fountain?
Meanwhile the editorial They—
who are no less powerful—
prepare to smother the actual Us
with a processed flow of all our shit
nonverbal.

Have you ever risen in the night
bursting with knowledge and the world
dissolves toward any listening ear
into which you can pour
whatever you knew   before waking
Only to find all ears asleep
drugged perhaps by a dream of words
because as you scream into them
over and over   nothing stirs
and the mind you have reached
is not a working mind
please hang up and die again?

The mind
you have reached is not a working mind
Please hang up
And die again.

Talking to some people is like talking to a toilet.

(1969)

CABLES TO RAGE OR I'VE BEEN TALKING ON THIS STREET CORNER A HELL OF A LONG TIME

This is how I came to be loved
by loving myself
loveless.

One day I slipped in a snowy gutter of Brighton Beach
and booted feet passing
me by on the curb squished my laundry ticket
into the slush   I thought fuck it now
I'll never get my clean sheet and I cried bitter tears
into the snow under my cheek in that gutter in Brighton Beach
Brooklyn where I was living because it was cheap
In a furnished room with cooking privileges
and an old thrown-away mama who lived down the hall
yente who sat all day long in our common kitchen
weeping because her children made her live with a schwartze
and while she wept she drank up all my cream soda
every day before I came home.
Then she sat and watched me watching my chicken feet stewing
on Fridays when I got paid
and she taught me to boil old corn in the husk
to make it taste green and fresh.

There were not many pleasures in that winter
and I loved cream soda
there were not many people in that winter

and I came to hate that old woman.
That winter I got fat on stale corn on the cob
and chicken foot stew and the day before Christmas
no presents to wrap
I poured two ounces of Nux Vomica into a bottle of cream soda
and listened to that old lady puke all night long.

When spring came I crossed the river again
moving up in the world six and a half stories
and one day on the corner of Eighth street
across from Wanamakers
which had burned down while I was away in Brooklyn—
where I caught the bus to work
a bus driver slowed down at the bus stop one morning—
I was late   it was raining   my jacket was soaked—
then speeded past without stopping when he saw my face.

I have been given other doses of truth—
that particular form of annihilation—
shot through by the cold eye of the way things are baby
and left for dead on a hundred streets of this city
but oh that captain marvel glance
brushing up against my skull like a steel bar
in passing
and my heart withered sheets in the gutter
passing passing
booted feet and bus drivers
old yentes in Brighton Beach kitchens

SHIT! said the king and the whole court strained
passing   me
out as an ill-tempered wind
lashing around the corner
of 125th Street and Lenox.

(1969)

RELEASE TIME

I came to their white   terror first
shackled
nuns with their ghostly motives
hidden in black   motionless
yet always upon us before we sinned
knowing   and smiling
sadly.

The neat sample loaves
of stale Silvercup Bread
and free lukewarm milk
in the chalky afternoons
the threat of public school
always   hanging over us
making me want to believe
the slight faces of magic
marooned in an ocean of Black.

I pray to almighty god to
blessed michael the archangel   defend us
in battle   be our protection
against the wickedness and snares of
the devil who comes   white-robed
to our daily crucifixions

restrain him oh lord we beseech and implore
you   who shall not hear us
praying again   except to seek
in ourselves   what is most human
to sustain us
and less terror
for our children.

(1969)

BALLAD FROM
CHILDHOOD

Mommy mommy come and see
what the strawmen left for me
in our land of ice and house of snow
I have found a seed to grow
Mommy may I plant a tree?

What the eyes don't see the heart don't hurt.

Mommy look the seed has wings
my tree might call a bird that sings . . .
the strawmen left no spade   no earth
and ice will not bring my seed to birth—
but what if I dig beneath these things?

Watch the bird forget but the trap doesn't.

Please mommy do not beat me so!
yes   I will learn to love the snow!
yes   I never wanted seed nor tree!
yes   ice is quite enough for me!
who knows what trouble-leaves might grow!

I don't fatten frogs to feed snakes.

(1969)

NEW YORK CITY

I

How do you spell change
like frayed slogan underwear
with an emptied can of yesterday's meanings
with yesterday's names?
What does the we-bird see with
who has lost its I's?

There is nothing beautiful left in the streets of this city.
I have come to believe in death and renewal by fire.
Past questioning the necessities of blood
why it must be mine or my children's time
that will see this grim city quake   to be reborn   perhaps
blackened again   but this time with a sense of purpose;
tired of the past tense forever   of assertion
and repetition   of ego-trips through an incomplete self
where two years ago proud rang for promise but now
it is time for fruit and all the agonies are barren
only the children are growing:

How else can the self become whole
save by making self into its own new religion?
Yet I am bound like an old lover   a true believer
to this city's death by accretion and slow ritual
and I submit to its penance for a trial
as new steel is tried
I submit my children also to its agonies
and they are not even the city's past lovers.

But I submit them
to the harshness   the growing cold
to the brutalizations   which if survived
will teach them strength   or an understanding
of how strength is gotten   and will not be forgotten:
It will be their city then:

I submit them
loving them above all others save myself
to the fire   to the rage   to the ritual sacrifications
to be tried as new steel is tried;
and in its wasting   this city shall try them
as the blood-splash of a royal victim
tries the hand of the destroyer.

II

I hide behind tenements and subways
in fluorescent alleys   watching as flames
walk the streets of this empire's altar
rage through the veins of this sacrificial stenchpot
smeared on the east shore of a continent's insanity
conceived in the psychic twilight
of murderers and pilgrims   rank with money
and nightmare   and too many useless people
who will not move over   nor die
who cannot bend   even before the winds
of their own preservation   even under the weight
of their own hates
Who cannot amend nor conceive
nor even learn to share   their own visions
who bomb children into mortar in churches
work plastic offal   and metal   and the flesh of their enemies

into subway rush-hour temples
where obscene priests
finger and worship each other in secret.

They think they are praying when they squat
to shit money-pebbles   shaped like their parents' brains—
who exist   to go into dust   to exist again
grosser   and more swollen
and without ever relinquishing   space
or breath   or energy   from their private hoard.

I do not need   to make war nor peace
with these prancing and murderous deacons
who refuse to recognize their role
in this covenant we live upon
and so have come to fear   and despise
even their own children;
but I condemn myself
and my loves   past and present
and the blessed enthusiasms of all my children
to this city   without reason or future
without hope   to be tried
as the new steel is tried
before trusted to slaughter.

I walk down the withering limbs
of New York   my last discarded house
and there is nothing worth salvage left in this city
but faint reedy voices   like echoes
of once beautiful children.

(1971)

TO THE GIRL WHO LIVES
IN A TREE

A letter in my mailbox says you've made it
to Honduras and I wonder   what is the color
of the wood you are chopping now.

When you left this city I wept for a year
down 14th Street across the Taconic Parkway
through the shingled birdcotes along Riverside Drive
but I was glad   because in your going
you left me a new country
where Riverside Drive became an embattlement
even dynamite could not blast free
where making both love and war
became less inconsistent
and as my tears watered morning   I became
my own place to fathom.

While part of me follows you still
thru the woods of Oregon
splitting dead wood with a rusty axe
acting out the nightmares of your mothers'
creamy skin soot-covered from communal fires
where you provide   and labor
to discipline your dreams
whose symbols are immortalized
in lies of history   told like fairy tales
called power   behind the throne
called noble frontier drudge and
we both know you are not white

with rage or fury   only
from bleeding too much while trudging
behind a wagon   and confidentially
did you really conquer Donner Pass
with only a handcart?

My mothers' nightmares are not yours
but just as binding.
If in your sleep you tasted a child's blood
behind your teeth
while your chained black hand could not rise
to wipe away his death upon your lips
perhaps you would consider why
I choose brick and shitty stone
over the good earth's challenge of green.

Your mothers' nightmares are not mine
but just as binding.
And we share more than a trap
between our legs
where long game howl
back and forth across country
finding less than what they bargained for
but more than they ever feared
so dreams or not   you will be back soon
from Honduras   where the woods are even thicker
than in Oregon.
You will make a choice too
between loving women or loving trees
and if only from the standpoint of free movement
women win   hands down.

(1971)

HARD LOVE
ROCK II

Listen brother   love you
love you   love you   love you
dig me
a different colored grave
we are both lying
side by side   in the same place
where you put me   down
deeper still   we are
aloneness
unresolved by weeping
sacked cities   not rebuilt
by slogans   by rhetorical pricks
picking the lock
that has always been   open.

Black is
not beautiful   baby
beautiful baby   beautiful
let's do it again
It is

not being screwed twice
at the same time
from on top   as well as
from my side.

(1971)

LOVE POEM

Speak earth and bless me
with what is richest
make sky flow honey out of my hips
rigid as mountains
spread over a valley
carved out by the mouth of rain.

And I knew when I entered her   I was
high wind in her forest's hollow
fingers whispering sound
honey flowed   from the split cup
impaled on a lance of tongues
on the tips of her breasts   on her navel
and my breath   howling into her entrances
through lungs of pain.

Greedy as herring-gulls
or a child
I swing out   over the earth
over and over   again.

(1971)

SONG FOR A
THIN SISTER

Either heard or taught
as girls   we thought
that skinny was funny
or a little bit   silly
and   feeling a pull
toward the large and the colorful
I would joke you   when
you grew too thin.

But your new kind of hunger
makes me chilly   like danger
I see you forever retreating
shrinking   into a stranger
in flight
and growing up
Black   and fat
I was so sure that   skinny
was funny   or silly
but always
white.

(1971)

ST. LOUIS A CITY
OUT OF TIME

If a city
takes its rhythms
from the river
that cuts through it
the pulse of the Mississippi
has torn this city
apart.

St. Louis is
somebody's home
and not answering
was nobody shovels snow
because spring will come
some day.

People who live
by rivers   dream
they are immortal.

(1971)

TO MY DAUGHTER
THE JUNKIE ON A TRAIN

Children we have not borne
bedevil us by becoming
themselves
painfully sharp   unavoidable
like a needle in our flesh.

Coming home on the subway from a PTA meeting
of minds committed to murder   or suicide
in their own private struggle
a long-legged girl with a horse in her brain
slumps down beside me
begging to be ridden asleep
for the price of a midnight train
free from desire.

Little girl   on the nod
if we are measured by dreams we avoid
then you are the nightmare
of all sleeping mothers
rocking back and forth
the dead weight of your arms
locked about our necks
heavier than our habit
of looking for reasons.

My corrupt concern will not replace
what you once needed
but I am locked into my own addiction

and offer you my help   one eye
out for my own station.

Roused and deprived
your costly dream explodes
in terrible technicolored laughter
at my failure
up and down   across the aisle
women avert their eyes
as other mothers who became useless
curse our children   who became junk.

(1972)

THE BEES

In the street outside a school
what children learn
possesses them.

Three little boys yell
stoning a swarm of bees   caught
between the lunchroom window and a grate
Their furious rocks graze metal.

The bees are cold   and slow
to self-defense. One boy is stung
into quicker destruction.

School guards come
long wooden sticks in hand
advancing on the hive
they beat the almost finished
rooms of wax apart   fresh honey
drips down their broomsticks
little boy-feet   becoming experts
trample the rain-stunned bees
into the pavement.

Curious and apart   the girls
look on in fascination   learning
secret lessons   one steps
across the feebly buzzing ruins
to peer up at the empty grated nook
"We could have studied honey-making!"
tries to understand
her own destruction.

(1972)

A BIRTHDAY MEMORIAL
TO SEVENTH STREET

I

I tarry in days shaped like the high staired street
where I became a woman
between two funeral parlors next door to each other
sharing a dwarf   who kept watch for the hearses
Fox's Bar on the corner
playing happy birthday to a boogie beat
Old Slavic men cough in the spring thaw
hawking   painted candles   cupcakes   fresh eggs
from under their dull green knitted caps
When the right winds blow
smells of bird seed and malt
from the breweries across the river
stop even our worst hungers.

One crosstown bus each year
carries silence into these overcrowded hallways
plucking madmen out of mailboxes
from under stairwells
cavorting over rooftops in the full moon
cutting short the mournful songs that soothed me
before they cascaded into laughter every afternoon
at four P.M.
from behind a door that never opened
masked men in white coats dismount
to take the names of anyone
who has not paid the rent

batter down the doors
to note the shapes of each obscenity
upon the wall
hunt those tenants down
to make new vacancies.

II

These were some of my lovers   processed
through the corridors of Bellevue   Mattewan
Brooklyn State   the Women's House of D.
St. Vincent's and the Tombs
to be stapled onto tickets for their one-way ride
on the unmarked train that travels
once a year   cross country east to west
filled with New York's rejected lovers
the ones who played with all their stakes
who could not win   nor learn to lie
we were much fewer then
who failed the entry tasks of Seventh Street
and were returned back home
to towns with names like Oblong and Vienna
(called Vyanna)
Cairo   Sesser   Cave-in-Rock   and Legend.

Once a year the train stops   unannounced
at midnight   just outside of town
returns the brave of Bonegap and Tuskegee
of Pawnee Falls and Rabbittown
of Anazine   Elegant   Intercourse
leaving them beyond the tracks
like dried-up bones sucked clean of marrow
rattling with citylike hardness
soft wood   petrified to stone in Seventh Street.

The train screams
warning the town of coming trouble
then moves on.

III

I walk over Seventh Street   stone at midnight
two years away from forty
the ghosts of old friends
precede me down the street in welcome
bopping in and out of doorways
with a boogie beat.

Freddie sails before me like a made-up bat
his Zorro cape level with the stoops
he pirouettes upon the garbage cans
a bundle of drugged delusions
hanging from his belt

Joan with a hand across her throat
sings   unafraid of silence anymore
and Marion who lived on the scraps of breath
left in the refuse of strangers
searches the gutter with her nightmare eyes
tripping over a brown girl
young in her eyes and fortune
nimble as birch   and I try to recall her name
as Clement comes   smiling   from a distance
his fingers raised in warning
or blessing   over us all.

Seventh Street swells into midnight
memory ripe as a bursting grape
my head is a museum
full of other people's eyes
like stones   in a dark churchyard
where I kneel praying
my children
will not die politely
either.

(1972)

MY FIFTH TRIP TO
WASHINGTON ENDED IN
NORTHEAST DELAWARE

FOR CC—RING AROUND CONGRESS, JUNE 1972.

Halfway between the rain and Washington
as we stopped
stuck in the middle of Delaware and a deluge
At least she said
as the muddy waters rose covering our good intentions
At least she said
as we sat stranded neither dry nor high enough
somewhere over a creek very busy becoming a river
somewhere in northeast Delaware
At least she said
as we waited for an engine
to tug us back to where we'd started from
and my son complained he could have had more fun
wrapped up in an envelope
At least she said
as the flooded-out tracks receded
and the waters rose around us
and the children fussed and fretted but were really
very brave about it
and the windows started to leak in on our shoes
and the gum and the games and the *New York Times*
and the chocolate bars and the toilet paper
all ran out
as the frozen fruit juice melted
and the mayonnaise in the tuna fish went sour

At least she said
as the rain kept falling down
and we couldn't get through to Washington
as we slumped
damp and disappointed in our rumpled-up convictions
At least she said
The Indians Aren't Attacking.

(1972)

BARREN

Your lashes leave me naked in the square
but I have bled on prouder streets than these
so   my executioner   beware!
The song that haunts you through the trees
as you ride home to comfort
will not leave you at your door.

The warm maid brushing back her hair
who greets you with a kiss
knows my tune very well.
She hums it   under-breath
while your wine sours in the cup.

Smiling   she serves your dinner up
and need not ask what sound your ear
mulls over and over
like witches' laughter
nor whose sweet flesh
your rope cut in the square.

Her tongue   has tasted your death
many nights   and you asleep
beside her   dreamed me
your tormentor.

She and I
have come this way
before.

(1972)

154

SEPARATION

Stars dwindle
they will not reward me
even in triumph.

It is possible
to shoot a man
in self-defense
and still notice
how his red blood
decorates the snow.

(1972)

VIETNAM ADDENDA

For Clifford.

Genocide doesn't only mean bombs
at high noon   the cameras
panning in on the ruptured stomach
of somebody else's pubescent daughter.

A small difference in time and space
names that war
while we live
117th street at high noon
ruthlessly   familiar.
Raped of our children
we give birth to spots
rubbed out at dawn
on the streets of Jamaica
or left all the time in the world
for the nightmare of idleness
to turn their hands   against us.

(1972)

THE WORKERS ROSE
ON MAY DAY OR
POSTSCRIPT
TO KARL MARX

Down Wall Street
the students marched for peace.
Above, construction workers looking on
remembered   the old days
how it was for them
before their closed shop white security
and daddy pays the bills
so the hardhats climbed down girders
and taught their sons a lesson
called Marx as a victim of the generation gap
called I grew up the hard way so will you
called
the limits of a sentimental vision.

When this passion play was over
and the dust had cleared on Wall Street
500 Union workers together with police
had mopped up Foley Square
with 2000 of their striking sons
who broke and ran
before their fathers' chains.

Look here Karl Marx
the apocalyptic vision of amerika!
Workers rise and win
and have not lost their chains

but swing them
side by side with the billyclubs in blue
securing Wall Street
against the striking students.

(1973)

KEYFOODS

In the Keyfood Market on Broadway
by the window   a woman waits
daily and patient
the comings and goings of buyers
neatly labeled   old
like yesterday's bread
restless experienced eyes
weigh fear like grapefruit
testing for ripeness.

Once in the market
she was more
comfortable than wealthy
more Black than white
proper than friendly
more rushed than alone
her powers defined her
like a carefully kneaded loaf
rising   restrained
working and loving
behind secret eyes.

Once she was all
the sums of her knowing
more   somebody
else's mother than mine
now she weighs faces
as once she weighed fruit.

Waiting
she does not count change
Her lonely eyes measure
all who enter the market
are they new
are they old   enough
can they buy each other?

(1973)

A TRIP ON THE STATEN ISLAND FERRY

Dear Jonno
there are pigeons who nest
on the Staten Island Ferry
and raise their young
between the moving decks
and never touch
ashore.

Every voyage is a journey.

Cherish this city
left you by default
include it in your daydreams
there are still   secrets
in the streets
even I have not discovered
who knows if the old men
shining shoes on the Staten Island Ferry
carry their world   in that box
slung across their shoulders
if they share their lunch
with the birds flying
back and forth
on an endless journey
if they ever find their way
back home.

(1973)

NOW

Woman power
is
Black power
is
human power
is
always feeling
my heart beats
as my eyes open
as my hands move
as my mouth speaks

I am
are you

Ready?

(1973)

MEMORIAL III—
FROM A PHONE
BOOTH ON
BROADWAY

Sometime turns inside out
and the whole day collapses
into a desperate search
for a telephone booth
that works
quick
      quick
            I must call you
now
who has not spoken
inside my head
for over a year
but if this phone burrs
long enough
pressed up against my ear
you will blossom
back into sound
you will answer
must answer
answer me
answer goddamnit
answer

please
answer   this
is the last time
I shall ever call
you.

(1973)

AND DON'T THINK
I WON'T BE WAITING

I am supposed to say
it doesn't matter   look me up some
time when you're in my neighborhood
needing
a drink   some books   good talk
a quick dip before lunch
but I never was one   for losing
what I couldn't afford
from the beginning
your richness made my heart
burn like a roman candle.

Now I don't mind
your hand on my face like fire
like a slap   turned inside out
quick as a caress
but I'm warning you
this time
you will not slip away
under a covering cloud
of my tears.

(1973)

FOR MY SINGING SISTER

Little sister, not all Black
people are all ready
people
are not always Black
people
finding them
selves close
to how they see
themselves
being most important.

I see your friends are
young skinny girls   sometimes
tall   sometimes slight   sometimes
beige and neutral or mean or honest or weak
sometimes warm some
times even you
haunted by fat Black women who alter
like dreams in a shattered mirror
becoming   sometimes
tall   sometimes slight   sometimes
beige and neutral or mean
sometimes   even you
hiding in a bloodbath of color
as you slice up love
on the edge of your little mirrors
making smaller   but not safer
images of your sun.

Cherish your nightmare   sister
or under the cloak of respect
a fat Black witch may be buried
the silver stake
through your heart.

(1973)

MONKEYMAN

There is a strange man attached to my backbone
who thinks he can sap me or break me
if he bleaches out my son   my water   my fire
if he confuses my tongue by shitting symbols
into my words.

Every day I walk out of my house
with this curious weight on my back
peering out from between my ear and my shoulder
each time I move my head
his breath smells like a monkey
he tugs at my short hairs
trying to make me look into shop windows
trying to make me buy
wigs   and girdles   and polyurethane pillows
and whenever I walk through Harlem
he whispers—"be careful—
our nigger will get us!"

I used to pretend
I did not hear him.

(1972)

OYA

God of my father discovered at midnight
mother asleep on her thunders
my father   returning at midnight
out of tightening circles of anger
days' punishment
the inelegant safeties of power
midnight empties your house of bravado
passion sleeps like a mist
outside desire   your strength
splits like a melon
dropped on the prisoners' floor
midnight glows   a jeweled love
at the core of broken fruit.

My mother is sleeping
Hymns of dream lie like bullets
in her nights' weapons
the sacred steeples
of nightmare are secret   hidden
in the disguise of fallen altars
I too shall learn how to conquer   yes
Yes   yes   god
damned   I love you
now free me   quickly
before I destroy us.

(1973)

169

THE BROWN MENACE
OR POEM TO THE
SURVIVAL OF
ROACHES

Call me
your deepest urge
toward survival
call me
and my brothers and sisters
in the sharp smell of refusal
call me
roach and presumptuous
nightmare upon your white pillow
your itch to destroy
the indestructible
part of yourself.

Call me
your own determination
in the most detestable shape
you can become
friend of your own image
within me   I am you
your most deeply cherished nightmare
scuttling through painted cracks
you create to admit
me   into your kitchens
your fearful midnights
your values at noon

into your most secret places
hating
you learn to honor me
by imitation   as I alter
through your greedy preoccupations
through your kitchen wars
through your poisonous refusal
to survive.

To survive.
To survive.

(1973)

SACRIFICE

The only hungers left
are the hungers allowed us.

By the light of our sacred street lamps
by whatever maps we swore to follow
pleasure will betray us
unless we do what we have to do
without wanting to do it
feel enemy stone give way
without satisfaction
look the other way
as our dreams come true
as our bloody hands move over history
writing   we have come   we have done
what we came to do.

Pulling down the statues of rock
from their high places
we must level the expectations
upon which they stand
waiting
for us   to fulfill their image
waiting   for our feet
to replace them.

Unless we refuse to sleep
even one night in their houses of marble
the sight of our children's false pleasure
will undo us

for our children have grown
in the shadow of what was
the shape of marble
between their eyes and the sun.

We do not wish to stand
great marble statues
between our children's eyes
and their sun.

Learning all   we can use
only what is vital
The only sacrifice of worth
is the sacrifice of desire.

(1973)

BLACKSTUDIES

I

A chill wind sweeps the high places.
On the ground   bearers of wood
carved in the image of old and mistaken gods
labor in search of weapons against blind dancers
who balance great dolls on their shoulders
scrambling over the same earth
searching for food.

In a room on the 17th floor
my spirit is choosing
I am afraid of speaking   the truth
in a room on the 17th floor
my body is dreaming   it sits
bottom pinned to a table
eating perpetual watermelon
inside my own head
young girls assault my door with curse rags
stiff from their mothers old secrets
covering up their new promise
with old desires no longer their need
old satisfactions never enjoyed
outside my door they are waiting
with questions that feel like judgments
when they go unanswered.

The palms of my hands
have black marks running across them.

So are signed makers of myth
sworn through our blood
to give   legends
the children will come to understand
to speak out living words like this poem
knitting truth into fable
to leave my story behind
though I fall through cold wind condemned
to nursing old gods for a new heart
debtless   without color
while my flesh is covered by mouths
whose din keep my real wants secret.

II

I do not want to lie. I have loved other
young women deep into their color
who now crawl over bleached earth
bent into questionmarks   ending a sentence
of men   who pretend to be brave.

I am afraid
the mouths I feed will turn against me
will refuse to swallow in the silence
I am warning them to avoid
I am afraid
they will kernel me out like a walnut
extract the nourishing seed
as my husk stains their lips
the mixed colors of my pain.

While I sit choosing the voice
in which my children hear
my prayers   above the wind
I am afraid
they will follow these black roads
out of my hands   unencumbered
by guilty secrets   remembered sorrows
use legend to shape their own language
make it ruler   measuring the distance
between my hungers and their purpose.
I am afraid
They will discard my most ancient nightmares
where fallen gods become demon
instead of dust.

III

Just before light   devils woke me
trampling my flesh into fruit
that would burst in the sun
until I came to despise every evening
fearing strange gods at the fall of each night
and when my mother punished me
by sending me to bed without my prayers
I had no names for darkness.

I do not know whose words protect me
whose tales or tears prepared me
for this trial on the 17th floor
I do not know whose legends blew
through my mother's furies
but they fell through my sleeping lips
like the juice of forbidden melons

little black seeds sown through my heart
like closed and waiting eyes.

Although demons rode me
I rose up a child of morning
and deep roads sprouted across the palms
of my hidden fists   dark and growing.

IV

Chill winds swirl through these high places.
It is a time when the bearer of hard news
is destroyed for the message
when it is heard.
A.B. is a poet who says our people
fear our own beauty
has not made us hard enough
to survive victory
but he too has written his children
upon women   I hope with love.

I bear mine alone
in the mouth of the enemy
upon a desk on the 17th floor
swept bare by cold winds
bright as neon.

V

Their demon father rode me
just before daylight
before he could touch the palms
of my hands

to devour my children
I learned his tongue
I ate him and left his bones
mute in the noon sun.

Now all the words of my legend
come garbled   except anguish.
Visions of chitterlings I never ate
strangle me in a nightmare of leaders
at crowded meetings to study the problem
I move awkward and ladylike
through four centuries of unused bathtubs
that never smile
not even an apologetic grin
I worry on nationalist holidays
make a fetish of lateness
with limp unbelieved excuses
shun the use of pronouns
as an indirect assault
what skin I have left   unbetrayed
by scouring   uncovered by mouths
that shriek   but do not speak
real want   glistens and twinkles
blinding all beholders
"But I just washed them, Mommy!"

Only the black marks   itch and flutter
shredding my words and wherever they fall
earth springs up denials   I pay for
only the dark roads over my palms
wait for my voice to follow.

VI

The chill wind is beating down
from the high places.
Students wait outside my door
searching   condemning   listening
for what I am sworn to tell them
what they least want to hear
clogging the only exit from the 17th floor
begging in their garbled language
beyond judgment or understanding
"Oh speak to us now   mother   for soon
we will not need you   only your memory
teaching us question."

Stepping into my self
I open the door
and leap groundward   wondering
what shall they carve for weapons
what shall they grow for food?

(1973)

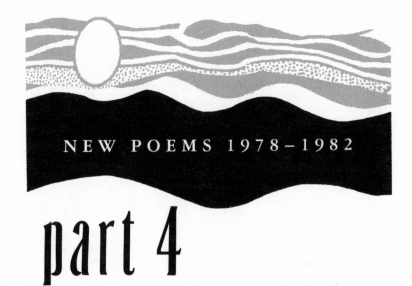

NEW POEMS 1978–1982

part 4

THE EVENING NEWS

First rule of the road: attend quiet victims first.

I am kneading my bread Winnie Mandela
while children who sing in the streets of Soweto
are jailed for inciting to riot
the moon in Soweto is mad
is bleeding my sister into the earth
is mixing her seed with the vultures' seed
greeks reap her like olives out of the trees
she is skimmed like salt
from the skin of a hungry desert
Ganvie fisherwomen with milk-large breasts
hide a fish with the face of a small girl
in the prow of their boats.

Winnie Mandela   I am feeling your face
with the pain of my crippled fingers
our children are escaping their birth
in the streets of Soweto and Brooklyn
(what does it mean
our wars
being fought by our children?)

Winnie Mandela   our names
are olives   salt   sand
like the opal   amber   obsidian
that hide their shape well.
We have never touched shaven foreheads
together   yet how many of our sisters'

and daughters' bones   whiten
in secret
whose names we have not yet spoken
whose names we have never spoken
I have never heard
their names spoken.

Second rule of the road:
any wound will stop bleeding
if you press down
hard enough.

(1979)

ZA KI TAN KE
PARLAY LOT*

Oh za ki tan ke parlay lot
you who hear tell the others
there is no metaphor for blood
flowing from children   these are
your deaths   your judgment

za ki tan ke parlay lot
you who hear tell the others

This is not some other cities' trial
your locks are no protection
hate chips at your front doors like flint
flames creep beneath them
my children are resting in question
so your tomorrows flicker
a face without eyes   without future

Za ki tan ke parlay lot
whose visions lie dead in the alleys
dreams bagged like old leaves
anger shorn of promise
you are drowning in my children's blood
without metaphor   za ki tan
ke parlay lot.   oh you who hear
tell the others.

(1980)

* Called in the streets of Carriacou, West Indies, before a funeral or burial.

AFTERIMAGES

I

However the image enters
its force remains   within
my eyes   rockstrewn caves
where dragonfish evolve
wild for life   relentless and acquisitive
learning to survive
where there is no food
my eyes are always hungry
and remembering
however the image enters
its force remains.

A white woman stands bereft and empty
a black boy hacked into a murderous lesson
recalled in me forever
a lurch of earth on the edge of sleep
etched into my vision
food for dragonfish   learning
to live upon whatever they must eat
the fused images beneath my pain.

II

The Pearl River floods the streets of Jackson
A Mississippi summer televised.
Trapped houses kneel like sinners in the rain
a white woman climbs from her roof into a passing boat

her fingers tarry for a moment on the chimney
now awash
tearless   no longer young   she holds
a tattered baby's blanket in her arms.
A flickering afterimage of the nightmare rain
a microphone
thrust against her
flat bewildered words
      "We jest come from the bank yestiddy
      borrowing money to pay the income tax
      now everything's gone. I never knew
      it could be so hard."

Despair weighs down her voice like Pearl River mud
caked around the edges
"Hard, but not this hard."

Two towheaded children hurl themselves against her
hanging upon her coat like mirrors
and a man with hamlike hands
pulls her aside   snarls
"She ain't got nothing more to say!"

And that lie hangs in his mouth
like a shred of rotting meat.

III

I inherited Jackson, Mississippi.
For my majority it gave me Emmett Till
his 14 years puffed out like bruises
on plump boy-cheeks
his only Mississippi summer

whistling a 21-gun salute to Dixie
as a white girl passed him in the street
and he was baptized my son forever
in the midnight waters of the Pearl.

His broken body is the afterimage of my 21st year
when I walked through a northern summer
eyes averted from each corner's photography
newspapers   protest posters   magazines
Police Story   Confidential   True
the avid insistence of detail   pretending
insight or information
the length of gash across the dead boy's loins
his grieving mother's lamentation
all over
the veiled warning   the secret relish
of a Black child's mutilated body
fingered by street-corner eyes
bruise upon livid bruise.

And wherever I looked that summer
I learned to be at home with children's blood
with savored violence
with pictures of Black broken flesh
used   crumpled up   discarded
lying amid the sidewalk refuse
like a raped woman's face.

A Black boy from Chicago
whistled on the streets of Jackson, Mississippi
testing what he'd been taught
was a manly thing to do
his teachers ripped out his eyes

his sex   his tongue
and flung him to the Pearl weighted with stone
in the name of white womanhood
they took their aroused honor
back to Jackson   celebrating
in a whorehouse
the double ritual of white manhood
confirmed.

IV

*"If earth and air and water do not judge them who are we to
refuse a crust of bread?"*
Emmett Till rides the crest of the Pearl River   whistling
24 years his ghost lay like the shade of a ravished woman
and a white girl has grown older in costly honor
(what did she pay to never know its price?)
now the Pearl River speaks its muddy judgment
and I can withhold my pity and my bread.

        "Hard, but not this hard."
Her face is flat with resignation and despair
with ancient and familiar sorrows
a woman surveying her crumpled future
as the white girl besmirched by Emmett's whistle
never allowed her own tongue
without power or conclusion
she stands adrift in the ruins of her honor
and a man with an executioner's face
pulls her away.

Within my eyes
flickering afterimages of a nightmare rain

a woman wrings her hands
beneath the weight of agonies remembered
I wade through summer ghosts
betrayed by visions
becoming dragonfish   surviving
the horrors we live   with
tortured lungs adapting
to breathe blood.

A woman measures her life's damage
my eyes are caves   chunks of etched rock
tied to the ghost of a Black boy
whistling   crying   frightened
her towheaded children cluster
little mirrors of despair
their father's hands already upon them
and soundlessly
a woman begins to weep.

(1981)

A POEM FOR WOMEN IN RAGE

A killing summer heat wraps up the city
emptied of all who are not bound to stay
a Black woman waits for a white woman
leans against the railing in the Upper West Side street
at intermission   the distant sounds of Broadway dim
until I can hear the voice of sparrows
like a promise   I await
the woman I love   our slice of time
a place beyond the city's pain.

The corner phonebooth. A woman
glassed in by reflections of the street
between us   her white face dangles
a tapestry of disasters
seen through a veneer of order
mouth drawn like an ill-used roadmap
eyes without core   a bottled heart
the impeccable credentials of old pain.

A veneer cracks open   hate
launches through the glaze into my afternoon
our eyes cross like hot wire
and the street snaps into nightmare
a woman with white eyes is clutching
a bottle of Fleischmann's gin
is fumbling at her waistband
is pulling a butcher knife from her ragged pants
her hand arcs back   "You Black Bitch!"
the heavy blade spins out

191

toward me   slow motion
years of fury surging upward like a wall
I do not hear it   clatter
to the pavement at my feet.

Gears of ancient nightmare churn
swift in familiar dread and silence
but this time I am awake   released
I smile. Now. This time is
my turn.
I bend to seize the knife
my ears blood-drumming
across the street my lover's voice
the only moving sound within white heat

"Don't touch it!"

I straighten, weaken, then start down again
hungry for resolution   simple
as anger and so close at hand
my fingers reach for the familiar blade
the known grip of wood against my palm
oh I have held it to the whetstone
a thousand nights for this
escorting fury through my sleep
like a cherished friend   to wake
in the stink of rage
beside the sleep-white face of love.

The keen steel of a dreamt knife
sparks honed from the whetted edge
with a tortured shriek

between my lover's voice and the gray spinning
a choice of pain or fury
slashing across judgment a crimson scar
I could open her up to my anger
with a point sharpened upon love.

In the deathland my lover's voice
fades   like the roar of a train derailed
on the other side of river
every white woman's face I love
and distrust is upon it
eating green grapes from a paper bag
marking yellow exam-books
tucked into a manila folder
orderly as the last though before death
I throw the switch.

Through screams of crumpled steel
I search the wreckage
for a ticket of hatred
my lover's voice
calling   a knife at her throat.

In the steaming aisles of the dead
I am weeping   to learn
the names of those streets
my feet have worn thin with running
and why they will never serve me
nor ever lead me home.
"Don't touch it!" she cries
I straighten myself   in confusion
a drunken woman is running away

down a West Side street   my lover's voice
moves me
to a shadowy clearing.

Corralled in fantasy
the woman with white eyes has vanished
to become her own nightmare
in my house
a French butcher blade
hangs   love's token
I remember this knife
it carved its message into my sleeping
she only read its warning
written upon my face.

(1981)

OCTOBER

Spirits of the abnormally born
live on in water
of the heroically dead
in the entrails of snake.

Now I span my days like a wild bridge
swaying in place   caught
between poems like a vise
I am finishing my piece of this bargain
and how shall I return?

Seboulisa   mother of power
keeper of birds   fat and beautiful
give me the strength of your eyes
to remember what I have learned
help me attend with passion
these tasks at my hand for doing.

Carry my heart to some shore
my feet will not shatter
do not let me pass away
before I have a name
for this tree
under which I am lying

Do not let me die   still
needing to be stranger.

(1980)

SISTER, MORNING IS
A TIME FOR MIRACLES

A core of conversations we never had
lie in the distance   between
your wants and mine
a piece of each navel cord buried
beneath a wall that separates
our sameness   a talisman of birth
hidden at the root
of your mother's spirit   my mother's rage.

Reaching for you with my sad words
between sleeping and waking
what is asked for is often destroyed
by the very words that seek it
like dew in an early morning
dissolving the tongue of salt
as well as its thirst
and I call you secret names
of praise and fire
that sound like your birthright
but are not the names of friend
while you hide from me under 100 excuses
lying like tombstones
between your house and mine.

I could accept any blame I understood.
Picking over the fresh loneliness
of this too-early morning
I find relics of my history

fossilized into a prison
where I learn how to make love forever
better than how to make friends
where you are encased like a half-stoned peach
in the rigid art of your healing
and in case you have ever tried to reach me
and I could not hear you
these words are in place
of the dead air
still between us.

A memorial to the conversations
we won't be having
to revelations we buried still-born
in the refuse of fear and silence
to your remembered eyes
which don't meet mine anymore.

Nothing
is more cruel
than waiting   and hoping
an answer will come.

I never intended to let you slip through my fingers
to ever purchase your interest again
like the desire of a whore
yawning behind her upturned hand
pretending a sigh of pleasure
I have had that, too, already.

When I opened my eyes I thought
we would move
into freer and more open country

where the sun could illuminate our different desires
and fresh air do us honor for who we are
but I have awakened at 4 A.M.
with a ribald joke to tell you
and found I had lost the name of the street
where you hid under an assumed name
and I knew I would have to bleed again
in order to find you

Yet just once   in the possibilities
of this too-early morning
I wanted you
to talk   not as a healer
but as a lonely woman
talking to a friend.

(1979)

NEED: A CHORALE FOR
BLACK WOMAN VOICES

For Patricia Cowan* and Bobbie Jean Graham† and the
hundreds of other mangled Black Women whose night-
mares inform these words.

> *tattle tale tit.*
>> *your tongue will be slit*
>> *and every little boy in town*
>> *shall have a little bit.*
>>> —Nursery rhyme

I

(Poet)
This woman is Black
so her blood is shed into silence
this woman is Black
so her blood falls to earth
like the droppings of birds
to be washed away with silence and rain.

(Pat)
For a long time after the baby came
I didn't go out at all
and it got to be pretty lonely.
Then Bubba started asking about his father
made me feel
like connecting to the blood again
maybe I'd meet someone
we could move on together

---

*Patricia Cowan, 21, bludgeoned to death in Detroit, 1978.

†Bobbie Jean Graham, 34, beaten to death in Boston, 1979. One of twelve Black women
murdered within a three-month period in that city.

help make the dream real.
An ad in the paper said
    "Black actress needed
    to audition in a play by Black Playwright."
I was anxious to get back to work
and this was a good place to start
so Monday afternoon
on the way home from school with Bubba
I answered the ad.

In the middle of the second act
he put a hammer through my head.

(*Bobbie*)
If you're hit in the middle of Broadway
by a ten-ton truck
your caved-in chest bears the mark of a tire
and your liver pops like a rubber ball.
If you're knocked down by a boulder
from a poorly graded hill
your dying is stamped with the print of rock.

But when your boyfriend methodically
beats you to death
in the alley behind your apartment
while your neighbors pull down their window shades
because they don't want to get involved
the police call it a crime of "passion"
not a crime of hatred.

Yet I still died
of a lacerated liver
and a man's heelprint
upon my chest.

II

(Poet)
Dead Black women haunt the black maled streets
paying our cities' secret and familiar tithe of blood
burn blood   beat blood   cut blood
seven-year-old-child rape-victim   blood
of a sodomized grandmother   blood
on the hands of my brother
as women we were meant to bleed
but not this useless blood
each month a memorial
to my unspoken sisters   fallen
red drops upon asphalt.

(All)
We were not meant to bleed
a symbol for no one's redemption
Is it our blood
that keeps these cities fertile?

(Poet)
I do not even know all their names.
Black women's deaths are not noteworthy
not threatening or glamorous enough
to decorate the evening news
not important enough to be fossilized
between right-to-life pickets
and a march against gun-control
we are refuse in this city's war
with no medals   no exchange of prisoners
no packages from home   no time off
for good behavior
no victories. No victors.

(Bobbie)
How can I build a nation
afraid to walk out into moonlight
lest I lose my power
afraid to speak out
lest my tongue be slit
my ribs kicked in
by a brawny acquaintance
my liver bleeding life onto the stone.

(All)
How many other deaths
do we live through daily
pretending
we are alive?

III

(Pat)
What terror embroidered my face
onto your hatred
what unchallenged enemy
took on my sweet brown flesh
within your eyes
came armed against you
with only my laughter   my hopeful art
my hair catching the late sunlight
my small son eager to see his mama work?
On this front page
My blood stiffens in the cracks of your fingers
raised to wipe a half-smile from your lips.
Beside you a white policeman
bends over my bleeding son

decaying into my brother
who stalked me with a singing hammer.

I need you. For what?
Was there no better place
to dig for your manhood
except in my woman's bone?

(Bobbie)
And what do you need me for, brother,
to move for you   feel for you   die for you?
We have a grave need for each other
but your eyes are thirsty
for vengeance
dressed in the easiest blood
and I am closest.

(Pat)
When you opened my head with your hammer
did the boogie stop in your brain
the beat go on
did terror run out of you like curdled fury
a half-smile upon your lips?
And did your manhood lay in my skull
like a netted fish
or did it spill out like milk or blood
or impotent fury off the tips of your fingers
as your sledgehammer clove my bone
to let the light out
did you touch it as it flew away?

(Bobbie)
Borrowed hymns veil a misplaced hatred
saying you need me   you need me   you need me

a broken drum
calling me   Black goddess   Black hope   Black
strength   Black mother
yet you touch me
and I die in the alleys of Boston
my stomach stomped through the small of my back
my hammered-in skull in Detroit
a ceremonial knife
through my grandmother's used vagina
the burned body hacked to convenience
in a vacant lot
I lie in midnight blood like a rebel city
bombed into submission
while our enemies still sit in power
and judgment
over us all.

(Bobbie & Pat)
Do you *need* me submitting to terror   at nightfall
to chop into bits and stuff warm into plastic bags
near the neck of the Harlem River
they found me   eight months swollen
with your need
do you need me to rape in my seventh year
bloody semen in the corners of my childish mouth
as you accuse me of being seductive.

(All)
Do you need me imprinting upon our children
the destruction our enemies print upon you
like a Mack truck or an avalanche
destroying us both

carrying their hatred back home
you relearn my value
in an enemy coin.

IV

(Poet)
I am wary of need that tastes like destruction.

(All)
I am wary of need
that tastes like destruction.

(Poet)
Who learns to love me
from the mouth of my enemies
walks the edge of my world
a phantom in a crimson cloak
and the dreambooks speak of money
but my eyes say death.

The simplest part of this poem
is the truth in each one of us
to which it is speaking.

How much of this truth can I bear
to see
and still live
unblinded?
How much of this pain can I use?

"We cannot live without our lives."

(All)
"We cannot live
*without our lives."**

(1979, 1989)

* "We cannot live without our lives." From a poem by Barbara Deming.